"Abasi Mu-Udim" The Creator and Creations

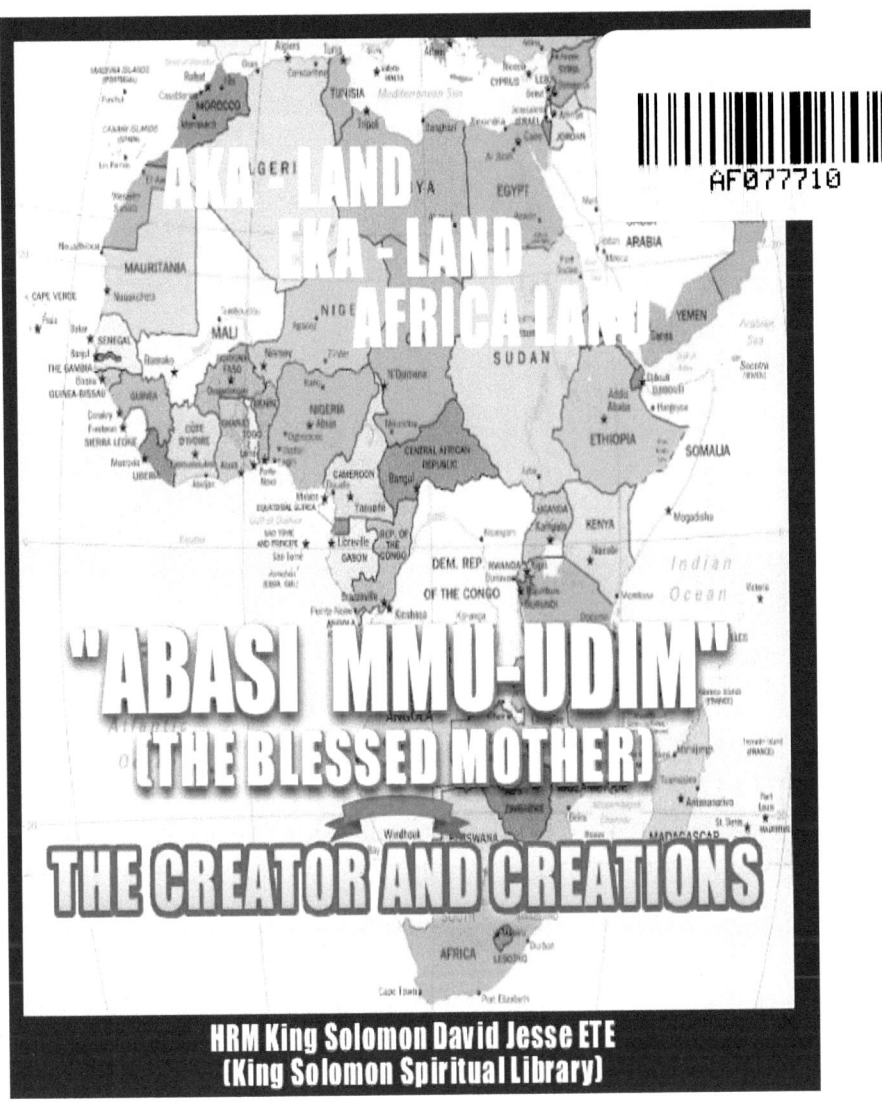

"ABASI MU-UDIM"
THE CREATOR AND CREATIONS

"Abasi Mu-Udim" The Creator and Creations

KING SOLOMON SPIRITUAL LIBRARY
THE GOD ENCYCLOPAEDIA WORD OF INFINITY

BY
THE SPIRIT OF THE FATHER GOD
THROUGH HIS SERVANT
HRM KING SOLOMON DAVID JESSE ETE
(King Solomon Spiritual Library)
Eteroyal Universal Family - BCS

"Abasi Mu-Udim" The Creator and Creations

All rights reserved
Copyright © Solomon ETE, 2008
Solomon ETE is hereby identified as author of this work in accordance with Section 77 of the Copyright, Designs and Patents Act 1988

The book cover picture is copyright to Solomon ETE

This book is published by
King Solomon Spiritual Library
P O BOX 27394
London E12 6WW UK
www.kingsolomonspirituallibrary.com

This book is sold subject to the conditions that it shall not, by way of trade or otherwise, be lent, resold, hired out or otherwise circulated without the author's or publisher's prior consent in any form of binding or cover other than that in which it is published and without a similar condition including this condition being imposed on the subsequent purchaser.

A CIP record for this book is available from the British Library
ISBN 978-0-9559801-6-9

Preface

As **I** always say, let every human heart be clean and clear and be with humility and with understanding with the love to hear from **THE FATHER GOD** once again. If you have that faith and belief then the communication between you and **I** will flow very well. But if you withhold your heart from **ME THE FATHER GOD** and hide yourself by having a double mind and doubting and not believing in **ME**, then the communication of understanding will be influenced by your thoughts as you do not believe **THE FATHER GOD**. That is the reason **I** bring all manners of information and all manners of explanations about **THE FATHER'S TALK (GOD PRESENT)**.

I want you to believe that **THE FATHER'S TALK (GOD PRESENT)** information is NOT motivated by cunning or by the human mind. It is NOT the WORD from the studio of carnality. It is NOT broadcasted by evil or by the second thought of a human being. **THE FATHER'S TALK (GOD PRESENT)** information is a direct broadcast, straight from **THE FATHER GOD**. It is broadcasted directly from the studio of **THE FATHER GOD ALMIGHTY THE SUPREME WORD OF THE UNIVERSE**.

All **THE FATHER'S TALK (GOD PRESENT)** Lectures Revelations are direct from **THE FATHER GOD ALMIGHTY**. That is why **I** call this one **BEYOND THE HUMAN KNOW**.

When **I** exist **I** was, was, was and this information existed with **ME** and that means that indirectly, **THE FATHER GOD ALMIGHTY THE SUPREME WORD OF THE UNIVERSE** is revealing **HIMSELF** to humankind once again. **I** do this so that you would not continue to think that **THE FATHER GOD** does not speak with human beings directly anymore. And most importantly this **FATHER'S TALK** (**GOD PRESENT**) Lecture Revelations are NOT given via any angel. They are not inspirational outcome from one possessed by an angel or a ghost. They are directly from **THE FATHER GOD'S** possessing heart in that **I** TAKE OVER THE BODY, THE SOUL AND SPIRIT OF HRM KING SOLOMON DAVID JESSE ETE AND **I** TALK THROUGH HIM.

This book is title: ***The Spiritual General Manuals of Life*** "**THE ADMINISTRATOR**" as the key and **ENHANCEMENT** of the **GENERAL DIRECTIVE** and **MANUAL** to be used in governing the whole world.

Contents

CHAPTER ONE   *11-143*

"MU-UDIM" THE BLESSED MOTHER

Part One   *11-62*

INTRODUCTION

Part Two   *63-99*

THE SECRET OF WOMEN'S PROBLEMS

Part Three   *101-143*

OUR DIVINE SELVES THE HOLY SPIRIT THE SECRET REVEALED

CHAPTER TWO   *145-282*
THE CREATOR AND CREATIONS

Part One   *145-189*
"SPIRIT" THE FATHER GOD

Part Two   *191-239*
"THE NATURE" MOTHER EARTH OR MOTHER GOD

Part three   *240-282*
"MUNDANE" ARTIFICIAL OR MONEY

CHAPTER THREE   *283-319*
THE INSPIRATIONAL WRITERS

"Abasi Mu-Udim" The Creator and Creations

CHAPTER ONE

"ABASI MU-UDIM"

THE CREATOR AND CREATIONS

PART ONE

"MU-UDIM" THE BLESSED MOTHER FOR BLESSED WOMEN

FATHER'S TALK
(GOD PRESENT)

Christ Our Lord Twenty-fifth, Thomas, **FATHER** Two Thousand and Eight (BE.AO.BOOH) Saturday Twenty-fifth October Year two Thousand and Eight (25.10.2008)

In the Name of Our Lord Jesus Christ, In the Blood of Our Lord Jesus Christ Now and forever more

MU-UDIM
THE BLESSED MOTHER FOR BLESSED WOMEN

Today! It pleases **ME THE FATHER GOD THE CREATOR OF THE UNIVERSE, THE SUPREME LIGHT, THE SUPREME WORD,** to bring out this secret record. The Lecture Revelation today is to mark out the **BLESSED MOTHER'S RECEPTION ON EARTH.** The title is **MU-UDIM, THE BLESSED MOTHER FOR BLESSED WOMEN.**

INTRODUCTION

I always request from humankind that whenever you come across **THE FATHER'S TALK (GOD PRESENT)**, the direct **WORD** from **THE SUPREME LIGHT, THE SUPREME WORD OF THE UNIVERSE, HE IS THE FATHER, THE FATHER'S TALK**, you must humble your mind. Forgive one another. Make peace in your heart. Come down to yourself. Wherever you may have travelled to in regards to where your spirit has roamed to, you must come down because **I** know that many people stay wherever they are but they are not there at home.

In the human system there is a home and there is a distant home and you also have a travelling centre in you. You have a shopping centre, you have a high court, you have a school and indeed, you have everything in your heart. You have abroad in your heart, because all overseas countries are in your heart. And that is why sometimes you can see somebody around or you can stay in your house but you are not there in your house rather, you are somewhere abroad. Sometimes someone stays in the village but the person is in the township. Sometimes someone physically stays in the township but the person is in the village.

Some people go to where they call a church but they are not in that church because they are still in their houses. For instance, a man leaves his wife in his house with a male stranger and goes to church. Maybe the man is a preacher but he will not able to control his church because he did not take his heart to the church. He left his heart in the house as a result of thinking about what was happening between his wife and the stranger. As his heart was at home, it means that the preacher never went to church rather he was in his house.

Some people follow their money and remain in the bank. They never reach home. So many rich people do not stay at home because they stay at the bank where their money is. For instance when they win a jackpot or they make millions in a business deal, you will not see them sleep well or relax. Their entire mind is in the bank with their money, calculating what they would do with it. They never sleep well. Wherever your treasure is that is where your heart is.

I want you to bring your heart to this treasure. If you treasure **THE FATHER'S**

TALK (GOD PRESENT) very well and you understand that **I** have made the provision and the remedy for mankind to develop and to take evolution to *MASTERSHIP* which is the Higherself then bring your heart to **THE FATHER GOD**. The Higher consciousness is for humankind to know **THE FATHER GOD** through **THE FATHER'S TALK (GOD PRESENT)** Lecture Revelations. The progression is, from the **EVERLASTING GOSPEL** to **THE FATHER'S TALK (GOD PRESENT)**. You need to know that you have to come here which means that you must bring yourself to yourself. Wherever you went and wherever you are, come home right now.

Whenever you have a copy of **THE FATHER'S TALK (GOD PRESENT)** Lecture Revelations, make yourself come home to be inside of you. That is, bring your mind and everything about you home to you. Forget about what you have as your possessions and every other thing during that time.

Bring yourself to this **FATHER'S TALK (GOD PRESENT)**; to the **WORD** you are about to listen to or about to read so that you can understand. Immediately you have done that, then put all of yourself together and read **THE FATHER'S TALK (GOD PRESENT)**.

You will benefit greatly because even if you are sick, you will become well. Any problem you have will disappear while you are reading or listening to **THE FATHER'S TALK (GOD PRESENT)** Lecture Revelations with all of yourself put together. It becomes **GOD PRESENT** therefore all your problems are solved immediately. Try and see. The taste of the pudding is by eating.

Anybody that has any problems should pick up any of **THE FATHER'S TALK (GOD PRESENT)** Lectures Revelations, assemble yourself, concentrate and then read **THE FATHER'S TALK (GOD PRESENT)** Lecture Revelation. By the time you have finished reading, **I THE FATHER GOD** who is in your **PRESENT,** will solve your problems because, the **WORD** is **HE IS THE FATHER. THE FATHER GOD** is the **WORD. THE SUPREME LIGHT OF THE UNIVERSE** is the **WORD.** When you are reading or listening to the **WORD**, which means you are eating the **WORD** then you are eating the breath of life. You are feeding your soul. All illnesses around you will vanish. All sickness around your soul and around your spirit and around your physical presence will melt away and you will become free! Because within that time that you concentrated and paid attention, you gave **ME** attention therefore **I** gave you **MY Divine** attention. Even with just one second of **MY** divine attention, **I** melt away evil.

Remember what happened to Adam's second temptation, when Lucifer turned to a beautiful woman to tempt him? He said to Adam, swear in the name of **GOD** who created you that you will do what I will tell you to do. Adam did not know it was another temptation and so he swore that 'in the name of **GOD** who created me, anything you tell me to do I will do'.

After Adam had finished swearing, Satan became satisfied that he had Adam again as before. Then he turned himself into a beautiful young woman! Sweet sixteen and naked! She said to Adam you see 'I am your new wife sent from heaven to you because your wife is old. She can no longer give you children.' Adam said to himself, "Again? Not this time around again!" Adam said to her okay let us pray.

As soon as Adam said, let us pray' that was the concentration that he gave **ME THE FATHER GOD**, for **MY Divine Attention**. He signalled by prayer that he wanted the **Divine Attention** of **THE FATHER GOD**. Immediately Adam closed his eyes and concentrated for communication with **THE FATHER GOD** and it took place, Satan ran away because she knew that Adam has connected **THE FATHER GOD**.

So, whenever you want to communicate with **ME THE FATHER GOD**, just concentrate. You don't even need to close your eyes. Just concentrate! Open your eyes and concentrate. One second of **MY Divine Attention** to mankind is more than one million seconds of any other attention, if you believe. If you concentrate for the purpose to communicate with **ME** that shows faith. That shows you believe. And that shows that you want to connect to the Divine Being.

This is not a matter of secret society knowledge. It has nothing to do with any such thing. And it does not need any ceremony. It does not need a ritual/s. What is required is that if you are annoyed; clear your mind of the anger. Come together with all of yourself in you and forgive one another.

At the time that you are connected with **THE FATHER GOD**, make sure that you have no problems in your heart. Free your mind and then give **ME** your attention. **I** will come as **THE SUPREME LIGHT** and give you **MY**

Divine Attention. One second of **MY** attention solves all your problems of physical life. Two seconds of **MY DIVINE ATTENTION** solves all your soul problems. That equals three seconds and your physical, soul and spiritual problems are solved for you.

This is the introduction to this **FATHER'S TALK (GOD PRESENT)** Lecture Revelation. If you can do this, then start to read or listen to **THE FATHER'S TALK (GOD PRESENT)**.

If somebody has to read to a crowd of people, let everybody give their attention by being humble, confess your sins and then all should be in silence – absolute silence. Concentrate and listen with rapt attention. Open your ears, your mind, your heart, your eyes and all. Every part of your body should be opened. All your windows of life should be opened to grip the information into your system, then all becomes well with you.

I always ask you to throw away your pomposity and arrogance. Throw away your high-horse attitude. Keep aside your high academic status and wisdom. Keep aside your prominent post and position. Whatever high or low status you have does not matter, as far as you are human being and breathe the air and speak the **WORD**, you are entitled to benefit from this. If you ignore any of **MY WORD**, then you ignore life. This is the only way **I** can return the whole of humankind to life everlasting by re-engineering your soul to live with **THE FATHER GOD** forever.

A: **IN THE REAL BEGINNING**

I AM going to give a Lecture Revelation titled, ***In The Real Beginning Of All Beginnings,*** which is the records of the **Real Beginning I** have kept till today. It may sound funny in the carnal ears but if you listen to your spirit-soul and humble yourself, you will know that **I AM THE SUPREME WORD**.

I AM the **ONLY ONE** that can tell you the meaning of **WORDS** of any language in any language. Every language in the whole universe means **THE WORD**. And it means only one thing, **THE SPIRIT'S** energy and the tongue. **I** interpret every sound. I can tell you the meaning of anything that drops and makes a sound. The sound from the human mind is the sound from the studio of **THE FATHER GOD**. The meaning of the sounds from any human being depends on the stages of the person's system. That sound is then the meaningful energy of that system. If your system is low then, the sound energy of yourself becomes low and meaningless and so lacks power. If you are higher in the system then you are also major in energy and that means that, **I** can decode any sound that comes from you and engineer it to become a fruitful thing that will benefit other human beings. That is the reason **I** call HRM King Solomon David Jesse **ETE** who is the original Abel, **THE BOOM OF GOD, THE MODIOBOM, THE INDEFINITE MEMORY OF THE FATHER GOD** because, that is where **I** store all information!

Anything of **THE FATHER GOD** is the soul of **THE FATHER GOD**. And when that thing is to manifest into physical reality, it manifests through a human being, because it is only in humankind that **I** can bury **MYSELF**. Humankind is a country. Humankind is everything because everything you see in this world materialized from human beings and that is why humankind is the image and likeness of **THE FATHER GOD**.

The money you see that everybody is using is a human being. The house you are living is a human being. The street on which you are walking on is a human being. Everything you see in this world is a human being. All the things you see are The **WORD** that manifested to what you can see. That is why the negative self, the back part of **ME**, uses what is called the spirit of witchcraft to operate because everything needs a human being. They use human beings in the soul to manipulate negativism. In the negative world, they turn every soul to be a slave. Those that go there know what **I AM** talking about. Everything is buried in the human being.

In the Kingdom of **THE FATHER GOD** there is no enslaving of anyone. Instead of humankind suffering, **I** make them Kings and Queens and Princes and Princesses and they are with love, with humility, with equality, with long suffering and with patience. **Humankind** should enjoy the privilege of being the **Image** and **Likeness** of **THE FATHER GOD**.

I AM bringing out this information of *In the Real Beginning* so that all women should have this knowledge because women are a very important phenomenon. Today! **I** want to decode that word, **WOMAN**. **I AM** also going to decode and give the meaning of the word of the English language called **MOTHER**.

MOTHER is not an original pronunciation and spelling of that word. What you call

MOTHER is part of the twisting of the tongue of words from the original formulation of all the languages in the world. Every language is a single **WORD** and **I** have the original records and the meanings of with **ME**.

The original language of **MOTHER** is **MU-UDIM**. **MOTHER** is actually a twist of the tongue of **MU-UDIM** and it means *mme udim* (multitude).

The **FATHER** means single. One thing is **FATHER** and **MOTHER** means **MU-UDIM** and that means plural, and that is many things, plentiful as creations. That is the meaning of **MU-UDIM (MOTHER)**. It is the twisting of the tongue in the English language that led to calling **MU-UDIM**, Mother.

MU-UDIM means plentiful and followers and it means creation. **WOMAN** means **MU-UDIM**. **WOMAN** means 'WE', **OURSELVES**. **I** will decode all that later in this Lecture Revelation so that you will know these things. This is *The Real Beginning* that **I AM** revealing now to all humankind.

B: I, THE FATHER GOD WAS ALONE AS A MALE SELF AS MYSELF

What the English people call **Male Self** means '**ME**', '**I**' in English. That is, **MYSELF**, alone. '**I**' is singular, nothing added and nothing subtracted. '**I**,' '**MYSELF**' singular, **FATHER**, **ALONE** and **CREATOR** is the meaning of **FATHER**. **Male-self** is a name without anything. It is singular, '**I**'. It is like being a bachelor. A man who is not married and has no child, sometimes is a virgin. That is the meaning of **MYSELF**. **Male-self** means man.

If everybody calms down and listens to this Lecture Revelation, you will have something to take to your soul that will make you to humble yourself before **ME, THE FATHER GOD**.

You can see that all men have made themselves to be Lords. They made themselves to look powerful and so control everything on earth! It is only because of **THE FATHER GOD** that made you behave like that. Let **ME** tell you, if **I, THE FATHER GOD ALMIGHTY** did not reduce the power of a woman you will be nowhere to found in the controlling of anything at all in this world. A woman is the most powerful thing on this earth that can control anything because a woman is not alone. She is with all creations.

A woman is a basket, a box and a drum.

A woman is a refinery tank and a nation.

A woman is everything.

A woman is plural.

A woman can never be alone; therefore, the capacity of a woman means earth. All things are included in a woman. It is only a man that is alone.

However, **I, THE FATHER GOD ALMIGHTY AM** both **MAN** and **WOMAN**. **I, THE FATHER GOD AM** everything! Without **ME, THE FATHER GOD**, which is **THE SPIRIT**, nothing and no one will exist. **I THE FATHER GOD ALMIGHTY AM THE SPIRIT** and **HE** is **NOT** only one thing, **HE** comprises of all.

Man however, is the one that is alone. That is why when **I** first created Adam as a father in the physical reality, as **I** revealed, he was alone. He could not do anything. He did not even know anything because He was alone. He was not a complete self. **A WOMAN AND A MAN FORM A COMPLETE SELF IN THE REAL NATURE.**

I AM talking about **NATURE IN THE REAL BEGINNING** in this Lecture

"Abasi Mu-Udim" The Creator and Creations

Revelation. **I AM NOT** talking about **SPIRIT**. **I AM** talking about **NATURE** on earth in the real beginning. **I AM** talking about what the meaning of **MU-UDIM** is, which is the word **MOTHER** in the twisting of tongue of the English grammar.

MU-UDIM is the real original Hebrew language. You may not find any Hebrew person now that can speak that original language because the original Hebrew is the land of Africa called *Akaland*. Africa was not called Africa in the beginning. It was called *Akaland*.

Akaland means *Ekaland*. *Eka* means **MU-UDIM** that is, **Mother**. *Eka* is derivative of *Ekara*. *Ekara* is from *ewet ekara*. *Ewet ekara* means [written] **O ekara**, *Ewet ekara*. *Eka* derived from *ekara* (round) *Ewet ekara*. That means the **EGG OF NATURE** that **I** broke and formed the earth was *ekara*, (**round**) and that point is, *Ekaland*. But because everything moves the way things move, **Ekaland** came to be called **Africa land.** But it was *Ekaland* originally.

Ewet Ekara that is, the **Ring land**, the land that was marked out as a Ring for **THE MOTHER GOD** as the landmark of the earth. Before Eve came, Adam was alone there at that time and then **I** created Eve to represent the completion of the land however that is not what we are talking about today.

What we are talking about today is how **MU-UDIM THE BLESSED MOTHER** blessed Her children and all women are liberated in reality from today because of **THE PHYSICAL RECEPTION OF THE BLESSED MOTHER, MU-UDIM.**

C: I PROJECTED MYSELF TO HAVE OURSELVES

I Projected MYSELF to Have OURSELVES called 'FEMALE' in the twisting of tongue of the English language. The word 'Female' in the English language was actually **FE, FEMASELF** that is **FEMYSELF**, which means, **Two As One**.

Female means, **Two As One**. That is, two things become one. That is, the half of the half put together becomes female. The first half was **MALE**. The second half was **FE**. And the two halves become **FEMALE**. Instead of **Fe** at that time, they said **Eve**. At that time after creation, I was not there to decode and tell them the actual words. It was the transit angels who brought these names to the earth that changed a lot of things. And the angel that brought these names to the earth dwellers and gave them this language is called ***Asiamimasiam.***

Asiamimasiam angel is called the **Angel Of Language**. That was the angel that wrote the scripts on the tablet for Moses. At this last dispensation **I** have not sent anyone. **I AM** here speaking directly to you. **I** can speak in **Efik** or **Ibibio**. **I** can speak in **Biakpan**. **I** can speak in **English**. **I AM** here giving you the true and correct information.

The name you pronounce as **Eve** is actually **Fe** (fé).

Fe was the original name and pronunciation but was then pronounced as **VE**. **FE** was turned to **VE** and then came to be written with another '*E*' before the '*V*' to get, '**EVE**'. Eve is actually from 'Even', the next of man that is, the next of kin, the next of man, the other part of man "**THE EARTH**". They all mean the same thing, but the real and actual meaning of 'Eve' is half-self. That is to say join this half with the other half to become one. The two halves joined together to be one and that one is called Vemale [female]. That is the 'male' self and the 've' self.

That was how **I** projected **MYSELF** to have '**OURSELVES**'. **VEMALE [female]** means '**OURSELVES or US**'. The single self is no longer alone. **WE** then joined together to become '**OUR**'. The capacities of '**US**' now consist of the **male self** and the **female** and the two became '**OURSELVES**' and so no more '**MY**' or '**I**' or '**ME**' but '**WE**' or '**OURSELVES**'. When you refer to yourself and another person together, you become '**OUR**' that is, two people as one, '**OURSELVES**'.

MY energy **Love** that is always with **ME** with the Second Thought, are the motivating factors for projecting **MYSELF** to do things. These ideas and formulations were not there when **I** did not yet make any creations. They were not there when the **Sound** did not yet occur. They were in silent phenomenon of **MYSELF** before the physical creations.

When you read the book *HE IS THE FATHER*, you will see that in the beginning, **THE SPIRIT** '**AIR**' was on top of the **WATER** and generated the **WATER** to form the **SOUND**. That is only what you could be told. Nonetheless, this is what **I AM** telling you now from **MY SELF RECORD**. **I** projected **MYSELF** as the Spirit gas and that is spiritual **oxygen** that you cannot see, you cannot hear and you cannot touch as **unseenable**, **unheardable** and **untouchable**. When **I** projected

MYSELF, I become '**OUR**'. That meant **I** wanted to make **MYSELF** plural. That was when **I** had **MY FE SELF** called '*Two-As-One*', **VE-SELF**, which people call Eve, in the physical world. Eve is the transit language from the angels that means '**the earth**'.

D: **WE PROJECTED OURSELVES TO ADSELF**

ADSELF is the original understanding of what is now '**OURSELVES**' or '**WE**'. This is where we understood ourselves together. When **WE** understood ourselves that **I AM** no more ONE, but **I AM** TWO 'OF US', it indicated that I had to make **MYSELF** plural. **I AM** now '**OURSELVES**' at referring to the **TWO OF US**. The question then was how do we progress from **OURSELVES** to **ADSELF**? It meant we needed additional energy to pluralize **OURSELVES**.

The original language to make **OURSELVES** plural is, *adian,* but in the twisting of the tongue of the English language it is '*ADD*'. *Dian* means **add** that is, **dian** or **add** this and this together. What is the meaning of *adian? Adian* means **add**. So, **adian,** *adiana,* **edian, dian** are all the same word **add** in different sentence contexts, as in **added**, **adding, addition** and so on. When one thing sticks together to another that is *adiana* and the plural form is *ediana*. Two separate things came together and become *adiana*. So, when *adiana* generated the energy to produce something that was when a '**CHILD**' came forth as a **SON** or **DAUGHTER**. A **Son** is alone '**single**' as another **father** in continuity process and a Daughter is plural as '**MU-UDIM**' **mother** or **expansions, multitudes** or **plentiful**.

The energy that resulted from the projection of **US –'OURSELVES'**, together is called *Adian Energy* and that resulted in *ADSELF*, this **adself** is what is known as the **Trinity Self**. **Adself** means **Trinity** and that is, **Adiana**.

There is no way that one thing that projects to form another thing cannot become two. And there is no way that two things that projected themselves together cannot become three. That is why it is, from the **Silent Thought** to the **Sound of Energy** and from the **Sound of Energy** to **Manifestation Of Creations**.

This Lecture Revelation called **THE BLESSED MU-UDIM, THE BLESSED MOTHER** is a real Secret Revelation that **I** have decoded for all human beings, and especially women to regain their glory that was lost. **I AM** giving this Lecture Revelation because of the physical representation of **THE BLESSED MOTHER ON EARTH** whom humankind received today. And that made **ME THE FATHER GOD** to happy and bring this Revelation Lecture that will engineer all women and all humankind both men and women to be happy! And they should be extremely happy! The entire humanity should celebrate until the world everlasting because the problems of **MU-UDIM** are finished today! When the problems of women are finished, the whole world is saved because most of the problems like negative traits, misunderstanding, and lack of patience and the rest of them hide under womanhoods to cause problems.

As **I, THE FATHER GOD ALMIGHTY** has decoded this today, the veil of ignorance has been removed from the entire humankind and humanity is free, in the name of our Lord Jesus Christ, *Amein*.

WE projected **OURSELVES** to *Adian Self energy*, called *Adian idem. Add Self* is also *Adiana idem* then **WE** became *Ita* (three) and that is *Tridem* (**Trinity**). *Tridem* is Trinity. That is the name in Ete Royal Universal Family that they called *Utinidem* which is also a result language and pronunciation variations. The meaning of *Utin* is not actually *Utin* but *Tridem*. *Tridem* means **IDEM ITA** (three self in one personality), UTIN-IDEM or TRI-DEM 'TRIDEM' **SUN SELF** or **SUNSHINE consisting of three majors things namely DAY, LIFE AND LOVE, NIGHT, DEATH AND MOONLIGHT, SPIRIT, WORD AND HUMAN. SPIRIT, BLOOD AND WATER, THE FATHER GOD, THE UNIVERSAL SUPREME WORD AND MU-UDIM 'MOTHER NATURE OF ALL CREATIONS, 'AKWA ABASI IBOM'**

People ask the involvement of **I THE FATHER GOD ALMIGHTY** with **ETE** ROYAL UNIVERSAL FAMILY.

'Why is **THE FATHER GOD** so involved with **ETE** ROYAL UNIVERSAL FAMILY?

What is the meaning of **ETE** ROYAL UNIVERSAL FAMILY?

What is the meaning of Solomon **ETE**?

What is this and what is that?'

People ask those questions among others about **ETE** ROYAL UNIVERSAL FAMILY and **I AM** going to reveal a part of that now so that you will know and another time I will give full revelation about womb of GOD on Earth.

In the whole world, there is nobody called **Utinidem**. And there is nobody on earth that understands that word, not even the people that answer that name.

The grandfather of David of Ikot-Okwo was called **Utinidem Akpan Esien Ibanga Okwo**. **Utinidem** is actually **Tri-idem (THE SECRET WORD)**.

This *utin* (sun) that you see to be so powerful is because of the energy of the **Tridem**. That is **MY Fuel Generating Force** in three capacities, **THE FATHER, SON AND THE HOLY SPIRIT**. The totality of **MY** energy produces the sun that fuels all humankind and also produces the air.

You can see that when the sun is very hot, it dries the water and produces dry air, and the water vaporizes and turns to become air. A miniature of this is when you boil water; say in a kettle or cooking pot. After a while, the water through heat application reaches a boiling point and starts to boil producing a hissing sound. As more and more heat is applied to the boiling water, it would produce a rapid and intense water boiling sound like *chooku-chooku-chooku!* As more and more heat is applied, the boiling sound intensifies because the energy has become very powerful. If the intense heat application continues, the water will dry up in the kettle or pot.

When it dries up, where does that water go? It turned to air. As the water has become air, the air will drop back to the earth as dew or rainwater. If the water is boiled in a closed room with no ventilation at all, when it all dries up in the boiling pot, the water will drop back into the dried pot again and you will see the droplets of water from the condensation that took place. That was how **Tridem** (**Utinidem**) was formed.

Tri Idem is, *idem ita adian* (three bodies added together). *Adiana idem! Ima Ete ye Eka adiana* (Love of Father and Mother together) Spirit *aduo asiagha idem ke ekara idem* (Spirit manifested **HIMSELF**) at *Ekara* land and that is Africa. Spirit *asiagha ke ekara* land and that is *Utinidem.* Esien means asiagha (rise).

Ebiet emi utin asiaghade (The place of sunrise) *Ebiet emi utin asiaghade edi Esien Idem (*The place of sunrise is *Esien idem) Utin Esien Idem – Utin Adian Idem.* Trinity produces life. That is, it is the sun that generates. **Utinidem** means the Trinity. *Idem ita adiana kiet asiagha utin.* (Three bodies as one manifested the sun). And this is the reason why **THE HOLY SPIRIT** has manifested on earth in The **TRINITY** form.

This information is not about a human self. It is about **ME GOD THE FATHER**, the manifestation of **ME THE FATHER GOD ALMIGHTY** in the physical manner from the time of original Adam. This is about the Natural Father Adam. And the same Adam was Natural Father Abraham. And the same Adam was Natural Father David. After Natural Father David **I** came as the higher Spiritual Father the total personified Word the Son of **THE FATHER GOD** the Higherself of ADAM, OUR LORD JESUS CHRIST. And **I** the Higherself of the Spirit came and met the natural self and that was at the baptism by John the Baptist who was the natural self. He represented the Water as MU-UDIM **THE MOTHER GOD**. And the **SPIRIT fire** represented **ME THE FATHER GOD**. And When '**WE**' both came together and sparked, '**WE**' produced the **Higherself** called **The Holy Spirit**, the Christ of **GOD**. And that is the manifestation of the **TRINITY GOD** now on earth as you are seeing now. That is why everything has become well for humankind.

Now! This **Akpan Esien Ibanga Utinidem** of Africa was the beginning of the ancestors. What you call the ancestors, the actual beginning, and the spot that the feet touched Africa. It is not for any human being.

What do you call human being?

How do you refer to human beings?

Some people do not respect human beings.

'Oh she is just a woman,' some people would say so dismissively of a human being.

Do you know the meaning of mankind?

Do you know the meaning of woman?

Do you know the meaning of man?

From today, be happy to find yourself to be a human being, especially if you are HUMAN-GOD! Even if you are a human-fish, a human-bird or a human-animal but you are positive, thank **GOD**! Because the only thing that is so wonderful, the most wonderful of all the things on earth are human beings.

When you see a human being you have seen **GOD**. When you see **GOD** in a human being that means you have connected to **ME THE FATHER GOD**, then you can see **ME**. You can hear **ME** and you can touch **ME**. Without humankind, how will you hear **ME**? Without mankind, where will you see **ME** much more touch **ME**?

THE SPIRIT you are hearing now talking or reading from is only made available to you because mankind exists. Without that, **I AM**

UNHEARD-ABLE, UNSEENABLE and **UNTOUCHABLE**. **I** cannot be heard. **I** cannot be seen and **I** cannot be touched. How will you hear **SPIRIT**? Where and how can you see **SPIRIT**? And how will you touch **SPIRIT**? Now **I** have become **heard-able, seen-able** and **touchable** because of the creation of mankind.

Utinidem Akpan Esien Ibanga Okwo. Okwo means completion. That is songs. **Father, Son** and **The Holy Spirit** put together are songs. You communicate with **THE FATHER GOD** in prayer, in word and in songs which means **The Trinity**. Song is the completion 'TRINITY'.

I manifested in, **Biakpan** which means the land of the First Son, the New Jerusalem. Then Bethlehem is where The **WORD** was born physically on earth. *Una node sabi somtin?* (Don't you people know anything?) *Una node hear something eh?* (Don't you people hear anything?)

Jerusalem is the City where the King has to rule. It is the City of the King of kings. Nonetheless, Jesus Christ was not born there. **HE** was born in the home of King David. That was where The **WORD** was to be born. **HE** was born in *Esien Ibanga. Esien Emana! Ibanga* is a twisted tongue of **Emana.** There is *Ibanga* and *Emana*. The correct meaning of *'Ibanga'* is **'TALKING OR PREACHING'** *Emana is* **GENERATION OR OFFSPRING!** So, the full names are **Utinidem Akpan Esien Emana IKWO OR IBANGA IKO IKWO (Okwo)!**

Emana ikwo (birth of song) *Emana iko Abasi* (Birth of **THE WORD OF GOD**) I hope Mfon will write this well. It should be written properly!

Akpan Esien Ibanga Okwo (EMANA IKWO).

Biakpan is the city of **Akpan (THE KING OF KINGS) OLUMBA OLUMBA OBU – Father - Adam**.

Ikot-Okwo the new Bethlehem is the city of **SONGS (THE SERVANT) DAVID – Son - Abel**.

They are the same land. It was not in another land. They were and still are in Africa and that is what I have re-established now in EKA – LAND (AFRICA)!

Biakpan and **Obio-Okwo (THE WORD AND SONG CITY** is the same thing as Father and Son, Master and Servant. IF YOU LIKE DO NOT FORGIVE YOURSELF! If you like hit your neck with a stone and not have mercy for your neck for your lack of love! That will not in anywhere affect what **I** have put in place spiritually.

So, if you as a father have a son and your son moved further away to establish his own family, is he not your son still? He will not live with you forever. He went and had his own place therefore that place is still yours.

Akpan had a problem, which **I** have now solved. **I** came from Heaven to engineer that.

If you go to **Biakpan**, you will know what is happening there. If **I** tell you the secret of **Biakpan** you will marvel. No human being on earth can withstand **Biakpan**. **I** mean **Biakpan** as a place. There is no place like **Biakpan** in this world. When you talk about something is something that is **Biakpan**. It is only **THE SOLE SPIRITUAL HEAD OF THE UNIVERSE** that can penetrate **Biakpan** – *Obio Akpan Abasi!* (City of the First Son of GOD) That is the New Jerusalem. And that **Biakpan** is **Calabar**. And the Headquarter of **Calabar** in spirit is **Biakpan** after **UFAN IMA (URAN) ABRAHAM AND DAVID**. Do you see **MY** business? **MY** business is like that.

Where you call bush today is where you will call township tomorrow because you do not know how things work. If you have lots of money and develop where you are, and there is nothing more to develop because you have reach a satisfactory point, you will look for some other uncultivated place to develop and that is what has happened now.

This was what made Cain to become jealous of Abel. If it is because of this **FATHER'S TALK (GOD PRESENT)** and how **THE FATHER GOD** talks about things that you become jealous of Abel again then, **I** will mark **X** on your forehead, just like **I** did at that time and you will kill yourself as you did before. So, you better repent and stop jealousy because everyone is not the same in gifts and talents.

Song:
  Stop jealousy
every man is not the same-o
Stop jealousy
every man is not the same-o

  It is only THE KING who knows
  *the secret of **HIS** kingdom*
  Stop jealousy!

  Stop jealousy
Every man is not the same-o
Stop jealousy
every man is not the same-o

*It is only **THE FATHER** who knows the secret of **HIS** kingdom*
Stop jealousy!

Do not be jealous like Cain who was on the side of evil. If you are happy about this Revelation Lecture, then you are happy about yourself because you don't even know where your link comes from. And you do not know the root you come from.

All roots of Abraham are positive and all roots of David are positive. If you therefore, come from the root of David and the root of Abraham then it means you are positive. Abraham had two sons. David had more than two. When you check all the children of David it was only one who was more positive. And it was the one that was linked to his father and that was Solomon who was Abel. Today! **I** have revealed how **I** projected **MYSELF**.

Now we projected ourselves ***Adian Energy*** *to **adself***, which is the Trinity Self, ***Tridem, Idem Ita - Idem Ita ke kiet, enye k'ekot* Trinity**. (Three capacities in one, is what is known as Trinity). It is not three separate bodies but **adian, adiana** added together to be three in one. When you bring two individual things and merge them, they become **a-one**, *adian* energy. And then that **a-one** energy produced the energy called *adiana idem, idem Ita, Utinidem Tridem*, that is the energy that produced the Holy Ghost. Abel produced the Holy Ghost. Abel was the first ghost because he was the first innocent human being that died and went to the land of ghosts. And **I** used that ghost to identify all positive children of **THE FATHER GOD** till tomorrow.

E: **IWEUS**

What is the meaning of **IWEUS**?
IWEUS is the first that produced Trinity as **I WE US**.

'**I**' is singular. '**WE**' is the two half. Then '**US**' is both '**VA-MA**' – (VM) family – **MU-UDIM.** All you have heard so far in this Lecture Revelation are still part of the introduction. As we progress you will see how lack of understanding was the root cause of all the problems. That is the reason **I** plead with you to humble yourself in order to learn and avoid problems.

If you listen to all **THE FATHER'S TALK (GOD PRESENT)** Lectures Revelations, you will learn and help yourself. Anything that is evil is bound for destruction. You cannot gain anything from evil. What is called evil is anything that is not a good thing. Strive to get what is good and totally ban anything that is not good. If you can, get good things from things and throw away what is bad.

Look at the Holy Bible. Why do you call it the Holy Bible? You call it the Holy Bible because there are lots of good things inside the Bible. There are words of love and so many other good words. Nevertheless, the Holy Bible is also filled with so many things that if you do them you will go straight to Hell. There are sacrifices and all sorts of unacceptable activities in the Holy Bible and all other directives from angels. Some contributions in the bible are from people of elementary understanding. Why then do you call it Holy Bible? Is it Holy? People use the Bible to do all sorts of evil, magic, invocations and all sorts of other evils. Nonetheless, it is still called the Holy Bible. The reason the bible is still called the Holy Bible is because there are lots of good things in the Holy Bible. However, all the people that use the Holy Bible for bad purposes **MUST** surely pay for their bad actions.

"Abasi Mu-Udim" The Creator and Creations

Therefore, you have to understand that if you have even one point, only one percent of goodness from anything then that thing is not totally bad. You can engineer that one percent to cover the whole thing to be good, if you have love and patience. That is why **I** stayed put from taking action to destroy human beings. **I** would have destroyed the whole of humanity completely. As people shout and say women are the cause of problems in this world then **I** would have destroyed women. And women say that men are the problem of this world then, **I** would have destroyed the men. And also that money is the root cause of problems then **I** would make money not to be available anymore. However, none of these things are problems.

The problem is your heart in regards to the elementary self that you still operate through lack of understanding which makes you speak negative words in the manner in which you do. That is why **I** have had a long, long patience till today so as to bring mankind back to the correct track. And when you have awareness and understanding of yourself then, everything becomes well for your soul. Therefore, **IWEUS** is the Complete Self that makes **PERFECT**. **I** can no longer say **I** alone or even **'OURSELVES'** for **MOTHER** and **FATHER** but **IWEUS**. I said **IWEUS** meaning 'Let **US**' create man in our own image and likeness. And from Let **US** create man in **OUR** own image and **OUR** own likeness misunderstanding started.

I would have said Let **ME** create man or Let **WE** create man but **I** said no, instead let **US** as **IWEUS**, so that man will be Trinity: **IWEUS** that is, **YOU, ME** and **OUR CHILDREN** and others and that is the same thing as **LOVE YE ONE ANOTHER** but in a more divine way. **LOVE ONE AND ANOTHER.** When you love yourself, you love somebody and you love everybody. That is what it is. **LOVE ONE ANOTHER. LET US CREATE MAN IN OUR OWN IMAGE AND LIKENESS**, so, **IWEUS** is the Trinity in you, **THE FATHER, THE SON** and **THE SPIRIT**; the **SPIRIT**, the **WORD** and **YOU** that is, your soul as the three in you. And that is **UTINIDEM** as, **Idem, Ita** and **Tridem**; **Tri idem**-three persons in one is Trinity that is, **Idem Ita**. *Dian idem Ita. Ama dian idem Ita enyenofi **Tridem** and* that is why you see, 'he' was called **UTINIDEM**. That is, everything has become three in one.

Mother and Father are two and that is both of us – **ourselves** as **Fe** and **Male** = **FE-MALE** and that is, woman and man together become **OURSELVES**. And that is the power of a woman. As a result of that, the **NATURE** thought she had the power to override **THE FATHER GOD** and that was when her head started to be bigger than her hat. And that was when it all started. **SHE** started thinking that yes I am very powerful now. I control everything because Nature nurtures. She actually forgot that it was not the case because since **I** have to attach **MYSELF** to Nature to bring out everything; all manifestations take life from **ME** therefore **THAT IS EVERYTHING**.

Do you see the failure? That was where failure started. That was the arrogance, pomposity, tribalism, segregation, jealousy and envy that made human beings to fail. If you don't progress from that and return to **ME** you will fail again woefully.

Anybody that has jealousy, segregation, envy, strive, arrogance, tribalism, pomposity has failed. You must conquer all these things so that you would have the patience to wait to know **THE FATHER GOD'S** programs.

F: **THE FATHER, MOTHER AND SON**

I put '**THE**' there. '**THE**' mean **I**, singular. You cannot put '**THE**' for **MOTHER**. You cannot also put '**THE**' for **SON**. Without **THE FATHER, MOTHER** will not exist. **FATHER** and **MOTHER** are now '**OUR**' as plural then our **SON** is added to become **TRINITY** so we have **THE FATHER, MOTHER AND SON**.

The **SON** is the male and the female. People do not understand the meaning of the son. People say daughter but **SON** is more meaningful in spirit. The actual word for **SON** is **ON** as in to switch **ON** something. To switch **on** is to come alive as something that is pulsating and vibrating and that means that is it **ON**. To switch **ON** is to be **ALIVE** and that is the meaning of **SON** meaning **THE FATHER** and **THE MOTHER** is **ALIVE**. They are alive because of the **SON** = '**ON**'.

The original pronunciation of '**ON**' or **SON** was *ENO*. When people then, did not understand the language and the original meaning, they said '**Ono**', instead of **ON** so **Eno** and **Ono** meant **ON**. They called it *'Eno'* but it was not '**Eno**'. This was just as they put '**E**' to **Eve** that was **Ve** then **Fe,** they also put '**E**' to **on** and turned the word to be **Eno.** The meaning of '**Eno**' - **ON** is Gift and that is the meaning of the **SON as** what the **FATHER** and the **MOTHER** got because of their energy and love is **Eno.** That is the actual meaning of a **SON** as a child. A child is *eno* meaning **gift** but the actual original word was '**ON**'. That word '**ON**' is not an English language word. It is the original spiritual Ibibio and Efik which was the original Hebrew language. The word was '**ON**' but the twisting of the tongue produced **Eno or ONO-IDEM (a gift of self)**.

The **FATHER** and the **MOTHER'S 'ON'** became life as the plural life formed on earth because of the **SON**. When **I, AIR** did not yet go on top of the **WATER** to generate the **water** with **air**, there was no sound. But, when that generating energy took place, the vibrating energy of the **water** and **air** produced the **sound** and that **sound** formed the **Gen** of creation that formed all the meaningful words today in creations PHYSICAL NATURE. Then **I** put that into physical reality in human beings and human beings could talk. That was the gift. That is why when a child is born, the first gift is the name given to that child. That is the meaning of *eno*, as a **gift** in the English language.

"Abasi Mu-Udim" The Creator and Creations

The first gift to a human being is the name. The first thing given to a child at birth is a name. Some people even have the child's name before the child is born. The only thing you can present to your child, as a gift is a good name as the child's own name. That is *eno*. A child is a gift that **The Mother** and **Father**, have from **THE FATHER GOD,** it means **THE WORD**.

Due to **MY** first gift called *Eno,* '**ON**', **I** was **ON** in the physical reality as **THE SPOKEN WORD**. And the **SPOKEN WORD** represents **Mother** and **Father** at the same time. That was why **I** created the Tree in the Garden of Eden called "**IDEM**" (HUMAN PHYSICAL SELF OR PRIVATE PART OF A PERSON) and it bore two fruits, 'ON called Eno' with his energy power of '**DIONG**' that causes plural of **LIVES** as '**ETI-UWEM**' to generate indefinitely for good living life souls. And the other one called 'OFF as Ebo' with her energy power of 'BIAT' that causes plural of **deaths** '**IDIOK-MPKA** to generate indefinitely for bad and uncomfortable punishment of dead souls ending up in hell. And that is why if someone is '**ON**' he or she is **physically alive** but if someone is 'off', it is physical death.

"Abasi Mu-Udim" The Creator and Creations

I, THE FATHER GOD, THE SUPREME SPIRIT OF ALLTHINGS SPIRITUAL, took the **ON** part of **ME** to produce eternity '*LIFE*' for all positive souls for their spiritual continuity and **THE MOTHER GOD THE SUPREME CARNAL OF ALLTHINGS CARNALITY** also took the **OFF** part of **HERSELF** to produce eternity '**DEATH**' for the end all of physical carnalities. That is why you see death on earth. That is the Night and the Day in operations. During every day time, **I AM** fully '**ON**' for *general life daily renewal* and every night **I AM OFF**. What do **I** turn off? I turn off the energy that generates the **FE SELF** that is **OUR** energy that generates to produce the day. When **I, THE FATHER GOD** do not visit **THE MOTHER**, it becomes night. When **I THE FATHER** visits **THE MOTHER**, it becomes daylight. And when **NATURE** and **SPIRIT** are not in good terms the weather becomes moody. The weather will not be very bright. And that is what is happening in the whole world. Nothing is new.

I AM decoding and revealing everything. Exactly what you see is what it is. When you read First John Chapter four from verse fifteen to the end of the Holy Bible, you will see what **I** mean. *As He is, so are we in this world*. It is a very deep sentence. '**As He is, so we are in this world**' means that we must love one another, because if you do not love you are in darkness. You are under death. Everyone should take the Supreme advice of **MY** positive **LOVE**. Love that is made perfect cannot be fearful. A fearful love is not made perfect.

Lack of understanding and lack of maturity brought fear to **THE MOTHER** and that brought problems on earth. **I** will decode and tell you all about the origin of problems. Therefore, in **MY** Supreme System of **THE FATHER, MOTHER** and **SON, THE FATHER** is *THE SPIRIT*; **THE MOTHER** is *THE CARNAL OR MUNDANE,* then the **SON** which is the combined energy of the **FATHER AND MOTHER**, is **THE SUPREME SOUL OF NATURE** as *"THE UNIVERSAL SUPREME WORD"* which is both positive and negative. The **SPIRIT** and the **NATURE**, and the two of them "**ON**" themselves and produced the "**ENO**"- gift. The *ENO* of **THE FATHER AND THE MOTHER GOD**, THE SPIRIT and NATURE manifested the human soul through the energy of multiplications, flexibility and love, and brought **ON**, which is *ENO, UWEM*.

G: THE CREATION WAS A BLESSING TO OURSELVES THE *"BLESSED MU-UDIM"* THE BLESSED MOTHER

What is the meaning of *ENO*? *ENO* is the power and of the force of creation that is, **THE SPOKEN WORD,** the supreme energy of the Physical Manifestation, a **GIFT** as THE SERVANT OF ALL THINGS OF **THE FATHER GOD, THE MASTER, THE MAKER OF EVERYTHING. HE IS ENO. HE IS THE CHRIST, THE KING OF KINGS AND THE LORD OF LORDS.**

HE is the 'ON' the energy of **THE FATHER AND MOTHER GOD. HE** is **THE CREATOR. HE IS THE SUPREME WORD OF THE UNIVERSE.** As **I AM** talking now that is *ENO* meaning gift, **THE HOLY SPIRIT OF TRUTH.**

The best thing **I** can do for you is to broaden your intellect by giving you this recondite wisdom. **I AM** giving you these records so that humankind would stop killing themselves. The time shall come that nobody will know anything else apart from **THE EVERLASTING GOSPEL** and **THE FATHER'S TALK (GOD PRESENT).** Then your eyes will open and your mind will broaden so wide with the **Wide Angle** of **THE FATHER GOD**. Come to Wisdom. When you come nearer to Wisdom, you come nearer to life.

So, The Creation was a **Blessing to Ourselves, THE BLESSED MU-UDIM THE BLESSED MOTHER.** You are blessed today.

Today is a day of blessing, because **THE BLESSED MU-UDIM – ABASI ME UDIM** is giving blessings to all creations. As **I** said, the interwoven power of all creations means **THE MOTHER OF ALL NATURE**. As **I AM** giving you **ABASI MU-UDIM** now, when your tongue is correct, you should call and pronounce the name right. The name is **ABASI MMU-UDIM** meaning **GOD OF MULTITUDE, GOD OF ALL CREATIONS IN THREE CAPACITIES; IN SPIRIT, IN SOUL AND PHYSICAL INTERWOVEN IN OOO**.

How would you know all these without **ME THE SPIRIT OF TRUTH** coming to teach man all things? This is your civilization in **THE SUPREME FUTURE**. This is your renovation centre of information. This is the totality of everything! When you read this **FATHER'S TALK (GOD PRESENT)** Lecture Revelation and surrender yourself to **THE FATHER GOD, I** will remould you. I will create **MYSELF** into you. **I 'ON' MYSELF** as

'ENO' into you and **I** become [**Tridem-Usun Uwem**] *'UTINIDEM – AKWA ESIEN EMANA'*! Therefore, all creations were created as the manifestation as **THE FATHER'S SONS**, *Eno ABASI* (Gift of **GOD**) and *Eno ETE* (Gift of **THE FATHER**). That is why today **SHE** is **BLESSED MU-UDIM. THE MOTHER** could only be accorded **BLESSED** when she had positive children.

I will now tell you why misunderstanding came into things in the first place. When **THE MOTHER** did not yet have a child, she was not happy. That was when **she** rebelled against **THE FATHER GOD** but **I** have now changed **HER** NATURE. We will come into that later.

Everybody should be happy from today that this Lecture Revelation has come. Don't hate any human being. Don't be jealous of anyone. Practice Live and Let live. Be happy! Show love to everyone! Share what you have with everybody! And be positive! If you know that you have evil spirit in you confess your sins and deny that evil spirit openly and disgrace it and bury it then, that evil spirit will run away from you. Take evolution to positivism now, because it is only the positive people that will enjoy this kingdom. And the kingdom is the whole world in the *UNIVERSAL SUPREME FUTURE* with the **GREAT UNIVERSAL CHANGE** now in place. Now that all things are revealed everything becomes new. There is no more evil power again on earth.

THE BLESSED MOTHER now **BLESSES THE ENTIRE UNIVERSE**, and **I AM** now revealing **MYSELF** to all **MY** creations that **I AM ABASI MU-UDIM, THE FATHER AND MOTHER GOD OF ALL CREATIONS. I THE FATHER GOD, AM** not the **GOD** of alone, but **GOD OF A** to **Z, ALL** and **ALL, ALPHA** and **OMEGA**. And that is why you see **THE BLESSED MOTHER, ABASI MMU-UDIM** physically, with **THE HOLY SPIRIT OF TRUTH** blessing all **HIS** children.

CONCLUSION A: **BY THEN THERE WAS NO PROBLEM**

All this time that **I AM** talking about there was no problem. Did you hear in the beginning there was any problem? In the beginning everything was good! All creations from day one to day six were good and **I** blessed them. There were no problems because everything was good.

CONCLUSION B: ABASI MU-UDIM THE MOTHER GOD

I have already told you the meaning of **MOTHER** and that it is the twisting of tongue of the English language for **MU-UDIM**. Some other twisting tongues say the word *Mofat or Muda* and many other twisting tongues of numerous languages.

The actual word and the meaning you **MUST NOT** deviate from, is **MU-UDIM**. The explanatory and expansive mode is **MME UDIM**, but it is correctly written and pronounced M M U – U D I M, MMU-UDIM and that is **GOD OF MULTITUDE, GOD MOTHER**.

The actual meaning of **MU-UDIM** that is, **Mother** is the **womb** that brought out everything, **THE CREATOR**. That is, where the creations come from that is *Ubet unimkpo Abasi* or *itie unimkpo ETE* (**FATHER GOD STORAGE PLACE**), *itie mbono* (assembly ground), *obio* (continent, nation), *idung* (country, place of origin), *ufok* (House), *udua* is (market), *Emana* (birth) all of them put together mean **ABASI MU-UDIM, THE MOTHER GOD**. All creations and all natures manifested from that part of **ME THE FATHER GOD**

ALMIGHTY, MMU-UDIM. The **WORD** is the only converting mechanism of all manifestations as the energy of **THE FATHER** and **THE MOTHER**.

THE FATHER - FAT that is, **HER**, back, **THE FATHER** alone, but **HE** manifested **MMU-UDIM**. Everything comes from **THE FATHER GOD** and it is manifested by **MMU-UDIM ABASI**. When the father goes to farm or goes to work, he brings things to the home to the mother and children. People go out to struggle to earn a living but they take their earnings home. When you have a business, you also take your profit home. Likewise, it is here because whatever **I** do, **I** take it to keep with **THE MOTHER. THE BLESSED MOTHER** is the overseer. **SHE** is the IN-CHARGE of all nature. Everything comes from there and manifested by *'ENO'*, by the power of **THE FATHER GOD AND MOTHER GOD** energy called *'ENO'*, the 'ON' energy who is **THE SON OF GOD, THE SUPREME WORD OF THE UNIVERSE.**

So, **ABASI MMU-UDIM** is **THE MOTHER GOD, THE SUPREME NATURE OF THE FATHER GOD**, the energy of all physical creations. All these things are from **THE FATHER GOD**. Without **THE SPIRIT,** none of these things will exist. Therefore, you **MUST** understand that **THE FATHER GOD** is **ALL AND ALL, THE TOTALITY OF TOTALITIES. HE IS THE FATHER. HE IS THE SPIRIT.** But when that **SPIRIT - FATHER** projected itself, it becomes **THE FATHER HERE, THE FATHER THERE AND THE FATHER EVERYWHERE** which manifested the Natural part of **THE FATHER GOD** called **ABASI MMU-UDIM**, the **PLENTIFUL** and the **PLURAL** as **ALL** and **ALL** in the **PHYSICAL REALITY**.

CONCLUSION C: **KIET-A-KIET ABASI, ONE AND ONLY FATHER GOD ALMIGHTY**

This is where **I** will explain to you how **THE FATHER GOD** was alone that is, when **I** had not projected **MYSELF** yet to manifest anything.

When **I** did not yet project **MYSELF**, **I** was alone called **KIET-A-KIET ABASI, SINGLE,** and **ONE AND ONLY ONE THE 'SINGLE-TY' FATHER GOD ENTITY** without anyone, without deputy or anything. **I** was **UNHEARABLE, UNSEENABLE,** and

"Abasi Mu-Udim" The Creator and Creations

UNTOUCHABLE. SINGLE! Nothing added and nothing subtracted! The **'WHOLE'** as **ONE WHOLE OF EVERYTHING! I** was the Phenomenon that existed alone and from **ME MYSELF**, everything came to be. *YOU MUST THEREFORE, RESPECT THIS.* All creations, all spirits, all souls, all hearable creations, all seen-able creations and all touchable creations and all persons must know where they come from. All the heard and hearing creations must know where their ability to hear comes from and be heard comes from. All seen and seeing creations must know where their ability to see and be seen comes from. All touchable and touching creations must know where their ability to touch and be touched comes from.

That is all from **ME, ME, ME THE FATHER GOD ALMIGHTY,** *HE IS THE SPIRIT* **ALL THINGS**. And everything put together means **BROTHERHOOD**.

I AM THE FATHER GOD, THE KIET-A-KIET, projected MYSELF from THE KIET-A-KIET ABASI and have another formula self called "AD-DIAN - FE-WAN" AWAN or IWANG – GARDEN- FE-MAN- WOMAN- IBA-N "ADIAN" meaning adding or attach to IDEM – SELF – OWO - PERSON. IDEM meaning SELF or EDEN - EREN "EMA" – IMA – INEM - IDEM and E-MAN (LOVE) now **MY** projected ADSELF 'ADD' ADIAN together with **MYSELF** SINGLE-SELF 'IKPONG IDEM' mean **MYSELF** ALONE – *KIET* - "AKWA" becomes *IBA* or IBOM "E-RENIBA". ERENIMA YEW-ANIMA 'DIANIDEMKIMA'– EREN YE NWAN IMADIAN IDEM KIET EKEN KIMA- the ADSELF to manifest 'ENO' of GOD. **THE MOTHER GOD, ABASI MMU-UDIM, and I THE, KIET-A-AKIET ABASI and ABASI MU-UDIM** have the completed Energy to make the physical creation through **ENO, THE SPOKEN WORD** as **THE IMA (THE LOVE)** and that is the completion.

Then **ENO ABASI** is **AKPAN ABASI** (First **SON** of **GOD**) *IKO ABASI- edi ENO ABASI, Enyedi Edisana Spirit.* (**WORD OF GOD** is the Gift of **GOD. HE** is The Holy Spirit). And then **I** manifested **MYSELF** as the **TRINITY GOD**, which is **THE FATHER, SON** and **HOLY SPIRIT** as the completion. That was why **I** said everything shall pass away, but the **WORD** shall not pass away. Again **I** said everything shall stop, but the songs shall not stop. You see that! That means the beginning and the end is **THE FATHER GOD**.

That is that for Part One, in the name of Our Lord Jesus Christ. *Amein*!

Part Two

MMU-UDIM

THE SECRET OF THE WOMAN PROBLEMS

MMU-UDIM

Part Two

THE SECRET OF THE WOMAN PROBLEMS

In the name of Our Lord Jesus Christ, In the blood of Our Lord Jesus Christ, Now and forever more, *Amien*

Today! It pleases **ME THE FATHER GOD THE SUPREME WORD OF THE UNIVERSE** to give this second part of the Lecture Revelation of today called **MU-UDIM THE BLESSED MOTHER FOR BLESSED WOMEN.**

A: **I AM THE WORD AND I AM THE ONLY ONE THAT CAN DECODE THE WORD**

I AM THE WORD and **I AM** the only one that can decode **THE WORD,** and that is the meaning of what **I** said earlier in that it is only the King that knows the secret of his Kingdom. What secrets are in the Kingdom of **GOD**? What is the meaning of Kingdom? Kingdom means where the Anointed One is and King means Christ, the Anointed One. And what is the secret of that place? It is the decoded revelations, as the truth revelations. That is some of the secrets of that place.

When **I WAS, WAS, BUSY WAS**, it means when **I WAS** and there was nothing in existence apart from **MYSELF**. It means that nothing was in existence, but **I THE FATHER GOD** and that means that if **I** did not bring records like this, you will not know about them. From time to time **I** always come to reveal secret things to humankind especially now that humankind has come to the understanding of themselves therefore **I** have so many channels to properly store and preserve all the information because the present world is digitally operated. There is digital recording and other modes of storing information. There is also many ways of distributing information faster and easier than in the past, as well using upgraded methods for the information to work well.

Previously an angel would come with one revelation or another and appear to a human being, then the person would probably start to write in say, Arabic and as a result, lots of things would be lost in the translation. Also some information would just be cut out of the main information that **I** gave. If **I** gave you the true story of **MYSELF** during those days, you will only have one percent of all the information. Ninety-nine percent would be lost in humanity's ways of life. Today nevertheless, it is not like that because **I AM** giving the information directly by **MYSELF**.

Have you not seen the way they manipulated the Bible? They also manipulated the Koran including all other similar holy records but nobody can manipulate this **FATHER'S TALK (GOD PRESENT)**. That is the reason **I** call this information 'Lectures Revelations'. Nobody should go and give lectures on the **FATHER'S TALK (GOD PRESENT)** information again. They are available for everyone to access. If you read any and do not understand, read another up to seven different titles of **THE FATHER'S TALK (GOD PRESENT)** Lecture Revelations. Understanding will come to you before you are through. So, you don't need a preacher for that.

THE FATHER'S TALK (GOD PRESENT) Lecture Revelations are from **ME, THE SUPREME PREACHER** therefore you do not need a preacher to interpret any of them. What you need is to open your mind and humble and subject yourself to the **HOLY SPIRIT OF TRUTH**. When you humble yourself and have faith then, **I THE SUPREME WORD** as **THE RECEIVER** in and **THE STUDIO** in you will make the channel to be clear. If you receive this **WORD**, then **I** will make you to understand the language of what you have received. **I AM THE WORD** and **I AM** the only **ONE** that can decode the **WORD**. I have every secret of the **WORD** in **MY** hand.

I know what will happen regarding **THE FATHER'S TALK (GOD PRESENT)** Lecture Revelations. A lot of people will accept, but some will deny this information of **THE FATHER'S TALK (GOD PRESENT)** and those who deny **MY WORD** and die will eventually come back to take this information in its full capacity. That will be only if you come from **THE FATHER GOD**, that is, if you are a positive child of **THE FATHER GOD** but you missed your way because of who you mingled with and the bad companies that you kept. For example, some people that come across **THE FATHER'S TALK (GOD PRESENT)** would want to react positively if left to them but another person or people would say, 'oh forget about that thing. Is it not Solomon that sat down and spoke these words'? Show **ME** any writer or anybody at all on this earth that can sit down and write things like these!

HRM King Solomon David Jesse **ETE** is not even aware when the Lecture Revelation is going on until later when He listens to the recorded Lecture or reads it when it is transcribed.

THE FATHER'S TALK (GOD PRESENT) Lecture Revelations are not prearranged; nonetheless they are prearranged in spirit. **I AM** talking through Him as a speaker as **I AM THE SUPREME STUDIO OF FATHER GOD ALMIGHTY THE SUPREME WORD**. I decode everything accurately without *trankinsen, pakansampam, branking, brikinsen.* Everything is done *craskit, craskit asikraskit* and that means, correctly and accurately, *a-very* correct decode, to speak your grammar. So, **I AM THE WORD** and **I AM** the only **ONE** that can decode the **WORD**.

B: WHAT MADE LUCIFER BECAME A REBELLIOUS SPIRIT-SOUL IS LACK OF INFORMATION

That is another aspect of this Lecture Revelation **I AM** decoding today. Lucifer is said to have done this and to have done that.

Why did Lucifer do what she did? Do you think **I** did not know what was going to happen? Who is Lucifer by the way? Where did Lucifer come from? Who created Lucifer? How did she manage to be?

Lucifer is **MY Back Self**, the first object of the **FE**.

When **I** projected **MYSELF** to **female** part of **MYSELF** so that **I** would have **Eno**, and have plural selves through generating the energy of love, that was the **SPIRIT** called **MOTHER GOD**. But in this **MOTHER GOD NATURE**, there is an object soul called Lucifer, just as there is object soul called **GOD** in **THE FATHER GOD**. The Spirit Lucifer is the female part of **MYSELF**, male and female. That is, positive and negative.

This self, Lucifer is called weak. She does not have understanding and she has no patience and she cannot survive without the other **SELF** that is, **MY** energy. As a result she cannot live alone. If any woman claims that she can live alone without a male counterpart, she is lying. Mfon Etteh **I** don't mean you-o! Even Mfon Etteh does not live alone! She lives with **THE FATHER GOD**. Nobody can live alone without **WORD**. Nobody can live without the **FEMALE** part of **THE FATHER GOD**. There is something that that part of your life accomplishes therefore if you live by yourself without a husband or wife then something is missing.

When a woman says that she lives alone, it is erroneous. When a man says that he lives alone, it is also erroneous. You live by instinct. Though it may seem so on the surface, but there is something that keeps you going that fulfils the part of a male if you are a woman and there is something that also fulfils that part of a female if you are a man. And one day **I** will reveal what it is.

The completion of **THE FATHER GOD** is **MALE** and **FEMALE**. I projected **MYSELF** as **MALE**; I also projected **MYSELF** as **FEMALE** to make a **COMPLETION** so that **I** would have The **WORD** called **ENO**. And that is The Son of **GOD**, the Christ of God. Problem arose because there was not enough information for **MY Female** part called Lucifer.

That resulted in the misunderstanding that occurred in Heaven in the lower self. Everything was silent and quiet and so there was no flow of information because **I** used the energy to create Adam and buried **MYSELF** in Adam. So, during that Ministry Work in the physical realm, Lucifer stayed without information. She had no feedback. She became silent. She was alone. She felt that **I** deprived her information and because of that she had a second thought, which was negative while **MY** Second Thought is positive. That was the confusion that occurred in Heaven. And what was the cause of that? It was a half-self that caused that. She did not have the **COMPLETE SELF** to exercise patience.

What gives natural patience is a **COMPLETE SELF**. And what makes a **COMPLETE SELF** is to have **UNDERSTANDING**. When you don't have understanding about something as such make wrong comments about that thing then, you have made a mistake. When you make wrong comments about anything, then you have become a 'half-self' because from there misunderstanding sets in. That is what is known as error that is, Satan. Satan came out from misunderstanding. And misunderstanding brings problems and death. So, lack of accurate information made Lucifer became evil, as Satan because she rebelled but originally Lucifer did not mean evil.

As a result of that misunderstanding, her original self cut-off from **MY SPIRIT** and became a '**Sent Out Spirit**'. When you read the book titled, *HE IS THE FATHER* you will see all this in detail.

As she became a **sent out spirit**, separation started. That separation caused the fall of humankind from then till today because from then on, human beings have two selves operating in them. One part says don't and the other part says do. When you do what you are not supposed to do, then you have made a mistake and then death comes. When you do what you are supposed to do then you have no problems.

You have two selves in you and one disagrees with the other. These things are inside you. That is the reason why **I** said, there is nothing like Satan and there is nothing like Lucifer. Everything is from the entire of you as a human being.

You should pronounce positive words and correct yourself then that error would cease. If no human being on earth makes any mistake in the way they **THINK**, the way they **SPEAK** and have **LOVE** for everybody then you will see that there will be no evil again. All evil is generated from the mind which is the elementary self as the premature self. Misunderstanding is the cause of evil because that is what produces evil, Satan, demons, the devil and whatever else you call the spirit of error. Where did demons come from? Demons came from bad souls as the people that died without correction because they did not change their evil ways before they died, as such their spirits roam everywhere. They wander about because they cannot enter into the real *ESIEN EMANA*.

When you die and don't go back to the real *ESIEN EMANA,* the real **TRIDEM** that is, the Real Self of **YOURSELF**, then you have not gone back to *THE WHOLE* that is **THE FATHER GOD** where you came from so you become a frustrated soul. For instance, when you go out from your house and came back and can no longer enter your house then, you have become a roaming about person. Therefore, for you to go out and come back to your house you must practice love for one another. You must **NOT** kill. You must **NOT** be wicked to another life. If you are wicked to another life and kill, you would have gained the energy of a vampire as a vampire angel as the first man, Cain, that killed the first man, Abel. Killing makes you the disciple of Cain instead of the Disciple of Christ, which is to be on the side of **THE FATHER GOD**. That is, the caring side, the lifesavers as the savoir. When you are on Abel's side you are of the Saviour's Group that cares for life.

If you are on the side of Cain, you are on the side of vampire as the life destroyers. And your own life will be destroyed too. The above is the decoding part of this Lecture Revelation.

C: WHAT A WOMAN NEEDS BEFORE SHE CAN BE BLESSED IS PATIENCE

That is the reason **I** said that women's problems are solved today. As **I AM** giving this message, this information, this Lecture Revelation **I** put potency in it for women to have patience.

The nature of a woman is that they take what they see immediately. It is not your own making. From today **I** have upgraded women to their former state. When there was no problem, when the woman that is Lucifer did not think that **THE FATHER GOD** kept information

"Abasi Mu-Udim" The Creator and Creations

from her so she was okay. Lucifer believed that during that time of creation she did not have the attention of **THE FATHER GOD**. Because of that, she rebelled. She thought that Adam had taken all the attention of **THE FATHER GOD** because **THE FATHER GOD** went and lived in Adam. So, for her to come and drag **THE FATHER GOD** back to herself, she came and deceived Eve and Eve deceived Adam and as a result, **THE FATHER GOD'S HOLY SPIRIT** had nowhere to live again in Adam and that made Lucifer to be sent away finally also! **NO PEACEMAKING! NO PEACEMAKING-O!** A child that does not want his mother to sleep h will also not sleep. However, from now onwards, since understanding is established in every heart, life reigns. You must have patience to fulfil **LOVE**. If you don't have patience then, you cannot gain this spirit back into yourself. So, **I** have given the Energy Of Patience.

I, THE FATHER GOD have a long patience however she always comes back to say, '**YOU** keep quiet a lot! **YOU** allow things to spoil! Speak!' But it is not like that. The reason **THE FATHER GOD'S** patience is long is because **I AM** the **THOUGHT** as the engineering thought, so, **I** know when something is finished and when to start. But she does not know. Carnal things do not know the **SPIRIT**, yet it is the **SPIRIT** that maintains carnal things.

You see how young children behave. What do they know? All what they know is that they want to eat. How the food gets to the house they don't care. Even when cooking, you will be shouting to the child to keep quiet for you to cook for him or her. The child would not listen to you. The child wants you to carry him or her and when hunger comes he or she will still cry for food. That is the **Baby Spirit**. When you read the Lecture Revelation titled ***THE BABY SPIRIT***, you will see this. So, lack of understanding and lack of patience brings problems and that is the downfall of a woman, which is supposed to be the other part that makes a whole. So, today! **THE FATHER GOD** with **HIS** mercy has balanced that aspect for all women as the representatives of **MU-UDIM**.

Without **THE MU-UDIM THE BLESSED MOTHER, THE FATHER'S Glory** will not materialize 'edoho ete ke *uwak owo edi ubong edidem'*. (It is said, multitude of subjects are the glory of the king). And that is why if there were nobody at all in the world, how would **THE**

FATHER GOD be the **GOD** of multitudes? Without the mother giving birth, no father will have a child. So, *Eno* (gift that is, child) came out from the father and the mother, but it is the mother that actually gave birth to *Eno.*

You can see that **THE HOLY SPIRIT** is the **MALE** and **FEMALE** part of the whole system that brings love and unity to the family. So, everybody is now happy. And **I** have made everything new. Understanding is now established.

ENYE ODUDU ABASI MI OOO ZIM ZIM ZIM ASASSU POSITIVE POSITIVE POSITIVE!

D: **THE SPIRIT HAS NO PLAN BECAUSE THE SPIRIT ITSELF IS A MASTER PLANNER**

That was the problem. If spirit possesses you, spirit will not tell you what it will do tomorrow. It will just take you to that thing.

That is the problem that HRM King Solomon **ETE** always has. And that is also the problem any spiritual person has. Nonetheless, that problem is now solved because every single woman now has understanding that they must attach to a man or they remain a virgin. Also, all lower people have improved to become higher, therefore, from today, you have patience. You also have understanding.

What was the problem? The problem was, "why didn't you tell me?" Tell you what? Did **I** have plan. The thing just started. The thing just happened. When you do not turn on something, why do you ask why it is not turned on? When something is turned on, then it is on. You see that? So now you want to ask **ME** that why can't the day break before the day breaks? have you heard that kind of query before, like someone asking, why don't you make the day break before the day, breaks? The day, breaks by itself. Is it not so? '*Yes* ***FATHER***.'

It is twelve hours of the day and twelve hours of the night therefore, have patience. Now we are in the twelve hours of the night. When it is six o'clock tomorrow morning, then we enter the twelve hours of the day. That has been automatically fixed, but this physical representative of **THE MOTHER GOD** did not know that because she was an **object soul**. Nevertheless, the Spiritual aspect of **THE MOTHER GOD, THE HOLY SPIRIT** knows this, but this physical representation of **THE MOTHER GOD** that is, the **female** part did not know. She thought the **male** part kept information from her. She forgot that **I THE SPIRIT was** very busy with lots of spiritual creations. **THE SOUL part of MYSELF** had no time because of **the** busy schedule to manifests the object soul of creations. Then the **physical** part betrayed **THE WORD** and **THE HOLY SPIRIT** had nowhere to live again. **THE HOLY SPIRIT** left Adam and the world went back to darkness. That has been the only problem ever since until this last time that **THE HOLY SPIRIT** has come back, in the name of Our Lord Jesus Christ to reconstructs the world.

Therefore, **THE SPIRIT** has no plan and does not plan. **I** have no plan-o! For instance, I did not plan this Lecture Revelation that you hearing today. It is not as though **I** planed last week that we are going to have this Lecture Revelation. It just came out now. That is the way **I** do **MY** things therefore, if you have the spirit of **THE FATHER GOD**, you will always stand by and be steadfast. Have faith and humility. When **THE FATHER GOD** is on, you are on. And you are always on and waiting for **THE FATHER GOD**.

The current **I** produce is like the electricity power. **I AM** on twenty-four hours nonstop. It is just as you have electricity supply but that does not mean you should turn on all your electrical equipment in your house. There is some electrical equipment that you need to have on all the time in order for it to work. An example is a fridge. If you turn off the electric current to your fridge then, your fridge is not a refrigerator anymore. Another example is your air condition. If you turn it off, it will not function to dispel the cold air as it is meant to do. Nonetheless, there are other electrical equipments or electrical gadgets that you do not need to turn on for twenty-four hours therefore the energy of those equipments is off.

THE SUPREME ENERGY OF THE FATHER GOD, WHICH IS I; THE SPIRIT IS ON TWENTY-FOUR HOURS NONSTOP. The SON which is **THE SPOKEN WORD** must be on because you speak the **WORD** to connect to **ME THE FATHER GOD**. You speak the **WORD** to connect to **THE MOTHER GOD** so, from today mind what you say and how you speak. Speak from the heart of **LOVE** and from the heart of **UNDERSTANDING**. Have patience until **I THE FATHER GOD** answers you. **I** hear everybody and ready to answer everyone but when you have no patience that is when you have problems.

If Lucifer had patience she would not be in the abject position she is today. Lack of patience made Lucifer to become evil. All women need patience. To represent **THE BLESSED MOTHER** you need **PATIENCE**. That is what every woman needs. That patience will make you to become a proper mother because if a woman has no patience she cannot bring out children. If you have no patience you cannot marry. If you have no patience you cannot bring up a family because women suffer more than men in all capacities. A woman needs physical power of long patience in all capacities. However, there is something a man needs more also to have.

What a man need more is the power of **THE SPOKEN WORD**. The energy he has is the WORD, the information. Until **THE FATHER GOD** speaks, a man cannot hear and until a man speaks, a woman cannot hear. That is the problem. That was why Lucifer lacked patience and has that problem till tomorrow. That is also the reason a woman cannot conceive alone. When the Virgin Mary got pregnant and gave birth she did not do that alone. The same **MALE** part of **ME** called the Holy Ghost rested on Mary before she conceived. **I** passed that instinct to Angel Gabriel to carry out that act,

ABEL was the first Holy Ghost, but I THE FATHER GOD IS HOLY SPIRIT. If no male energy comes to a woman she can never get pregnant. That is what it is.

E: WHEN SHE WAS NOT YET THE MOTHER

What was the problem for her lack of patience? It was because **MU-UDIM** was not yet a mother. She had no child yet. There was no **ON**. Everything was silent. And because of that silence, the **Object Soul** of **THE MOTHER GOD** rebelled against **THE FATHER GOD** because there was no **ENO**.

MU-UDIM was not yet a **MOTHER** in the true sense because there were no manifestations yet. And when **THE FATHER GOD** went for the manifestations then the problem came. The first complaint was the question that 'how are we going to have children'? How are we going to become plentiful? How are we going to have this? How are we going to have that? Then **I** called her and said, "Let us create man in our own image and likeness." Do you think it was just going on about creation? It was her idea. She was the one looking for the creation in order to become a proper **MOTHER**, to become **MU-UDIM** (with multitude) to become a proper **MU-UDIM** so as to lay credence to her name as **ABASI MU-UDIM (GOD OF MULTITUDE)**. Because of that request **I** said; 'Let us create man in our own image and likeness', but when **I** finished creating man, she did not understand let us now live in man. That was where the problem came from so she became **Oxymoron, Disagreement** because of lack of patience.

As you can see now, what caused the problem was that **MU-UDIM** was not yet a **MOTHER** but **SHE** was **GOD OF MU-UDIM (GOD OF MULTITUDE)** in the Spirit of the Thought of **THE FATHER GOD**. Everything was there but she was agitating about when things were going to start and all the creations would naturally manifest. **SHE** wanted this to happen and wondered how this was going to happen physically since **SHE** represented Nature. And it happened the way it did because the **Son** as **THE CREATOR** must physically **SPEAK** the **WORD**. That was where the problem came from.

When the pronouncement was made, LET THERE BE THIS… all creations manifested, then **I** said let **US** worship the **Son**. And let us respect the **Son** because **HER** glory is **HER** child, **SHE** misunderstood all of it and would not accept what **I** proposed.

F: **THE TIME OF NATURE WAS LONG OVERDUE**

The time of Nature to materialize was long overdue and because of that **SHE** could not stand it anymore. This is the exact reflection of a young girl or a young boy for that matter, particularly girls.

When you have a daughter and she starts her menstruation, you have to be very careful with her. You have to know how to handle her because if not she will have a child without being married. That was exactly what happened. If you can learn from this Lecture Revelation, you can solve that problem.

Anytime the menstruation of your daughter starts, you must think how to handle her. Change the mode of training. Change interaction. Get closer to her and tell her the facts of life. Bring her to the awareness of **GOD** and to herself. Tell her about ***Eno*** (**gift** that is, child) that is, **on** because when the menstruation happens to a girl, she is ready to have a child. As soon as any man goes closer to her, they become **our** and two become one. The production that will come out from that is *eno* a son that is, a child.

A lot of girls go out and about with that energy flowing. And when that energy over flows and becomes overdue the next thing is that she would have a baby without being married. In some cases without even knowing who the father of the child is. That is what is happening all over the place.

In that overdue state, she would not have patience because nature will not wait again.

That sort of situation is also applicable to plants. If you throw a corn to the road, it will germinate. It does not matter whether you plant it well or not. Any seed you throw on the sand will germinate unless there is no sand and no water then, it will dry and die. But if there is natural sand that seed will germinate by itself because there is energy already attached to it. Unless air does not pass through that seed and that seed has not touched the soil then, it might not germinate. But as soon as the seed touches the natural soil at an open place where the air can pass through, then the energy of the seed is generated, therefore it is **'on'** for that seed. When it is **'on'** then, the seed will germinate and bring out the energy. And one will to go to the soil and the other will come up into the air to bring out the bud that will produce the fruit for future planting. That is the duty of **MU-UDIM**, the **MOTHER**.

The part that goes to the ground that is, the roots and the taproot goes to bring up energy to the soil from the **MOTHER** to feed the whole plant. At a point the seed that was planted to bring out the energy will die, that is death and the resurrection is the germination of that seed. That is what **WE** call **GOD OF MU-UDIM**. It is continuation caused by death and life that is, the energy that flows between life and death and continuity. In life there is death and in the continuation of life there is death then in death there is continuation life. Those are the three things that are involved with living. And they are the spirit, the soul and the physical.

When the **NATURE** was long overdue because it stood by to bring out the creations, **I** gave order that they should not eat the Fruits in the Garden of Eden. The fruits were there to be eaten but it was not yet blessed because it was not yet mature but the **MOTHER** went through the backdoor because **SHE** was looking for *eno* (child) because **SHE** wanted to multiply. She was looking for a child desperately so she went and grabbed that thing prematurely and that was the problem.

It is a similar situation to when your child wants to marry, but you say, oh no, you can't have this man, you can't, and you can't. The next thing is that the child would get pregnant because you don't understand nature or you forgot how nature works. Your refusal to understand and acknowledge that tingling of body and the energy that flows between life and death and continuity can create problems for you. However if you have that understanding then you plan life very well.

When your daughter starts to have menstruation, know that the time is up. As soon as you see the first month of menstruation, the second and the third, then the time is definitely up. What the **on** time means is that it is the time to have *eno* to be **on.** And when your daughter is **on,** she will germinate and bear a child and that is, pregnancy. Whether you call it unwanted pregnancy or unplanned pregnancy, it is **on** already.

G: EXERCISE OF NATURE IN A PREMATURE STATE

What caused all these problems on earth is **EXERCISE OF NATURE IN A PREMATURE STATE**. The instruction **I** gave that they should not eat the fruits in the Garden of Eden was to serve a purpose. As **I** did not yet bless those fruits in the Garden of Eden, it was unsuitable for eating. If **I** had blessed the Tree in the Garden of Eden, the negative parts would have fallen away and melted and left the good parts for eating.

That is the reason that if you see your daughter going about fornicating when she has just started having her monthly periods then, she is likely to have children without a father for her children. It is only when she has patience and knows how to handle herself then; she will be able to avoid unwanted pregnancy and having a child without a husband. That is what happens with nature, in terms of the wild and unplanned germination. Nonetheless, both will surely come to pass.

If you speak properly it will come to pass. If you speak carelessly, it will also come to pass. So, it does not matter how you speak. Every word that comes out from your mouth will fulfil for you whether you believe it or not.

So, don't speak with a premature mind. Think well and speak well. When you think you can engineer your heart properly then you can speak a meaningful word. Also when you have a second thought about your word then it means that you will speak well that is, speak in a mature way. If you are not mature in your heart and you speak, that can bring misunderstanding and you could commit more error. And that is why the **EXERCISE OF NATURE IN A PREMATURE WAY CAUSES PROBLEMS** for women. It causes problems for mankind.

Lack of love, lack of peace, lack of humility, lack of cooperation, lack of mercy, lack of kindness are causing problems in the whole world. So, if you understand yourself before you have **EXERCISE OF NATURE**, then you will have no problems. Anything you do prematurely and without understanding will always pose some problems.

So, all women teach your daughters the good ways. Also all men, teach your daughters well. Every woman should take a lesson on patience and understanding because with that you will have no problems. When you read the Lecture Revelation called *THE MASTERSHIP* or the

Lecture Revelation called *OFFICE CABINET AND FILE* as *HUSBAND, WIFE AND CHILDREN* then, you will know that your knowledge and wisdom need to adopt understanding as their secretary.

The Chairman is **WISDOM**, the vice chairman is **KNOWLEDGE**, and **UNDERSTANDING** is the secretary. If you **UNDERSTAND** things then you can be well organized. Knowledge without **UNDERSTANDING** is rubbish. Wisdom can never exist without **UNDERSTANDING**. Therefore, **UNDERSTANDING** and **WISDOM** make things fruitful. **UNDERSTANDING** and **KNOWLEDGE** makes things fruitful. If you have any of these two or both without understanding, you will make silly mistakes. Love without understanding does not work because there will be no **PATIENCE**. With **UNDERSTANDING** you can have **PATIENCE**. Some people pretend to love but without understanding the love will collapse. Anything you do without understanding does not work. **UNDERSTANDING** is the proof of **FAITH**. **UNDERSTANDING** is the fruit of **LOVE** therefore everything must be managed and understood then, **LOVE** will manifest the glory of **THE FATHER GOD** in you. That is nature and that is why before you **EXERCISE NATURE** you must allow yourself some maturity. Let your system mature. Reach the mature stage. Have **UNDERSTANDING** before you **SPEAK**. Have **UNDERSTANDING** before you do **ANYTHING**. Before you **LOVE** you must have **UNDERSTANDING**, if not so that **LOVE** becomes **HATRED**. Let everything you do be with **UNDERSTANDING** then all will be well.

CONCLUSION A: **ABASI IKPONG, FATHER GOD, THE KIET-A-KIET ABASI, THE SINGULAR SPIRIT**

    I AM THE FATHER GOD in spirit but **I, THE FATHER GOD**, is alone. But **WE, US** together **THE FATHER, THE SON AND THE MOTHER** together **WE** become **IWEUS**. So, today, this is not the time of **ABASI IKPONG**. It is the time of **ABASI MU-UDIM**.
    ABASI MU-UDIM is the entire **NATURAL PHENOMENON** put together and they are called **MOTHER GOD THE SUPREME NATURE**.

ABASI MU-UDIM is **THE MOTHER OF EVERYTHING** that you see as all physical things and all are giving Glory to **THE FATHER GOD**. Everything on earth gives glory to **THE FATHER GOD THE CREATOR** so, **THE CREATOR** is in-charge but how would that manifest glory if **ABASI MU-UDIM** is not there. And for this reason there is multiplication formula.

Multiplication formula is the basis of mathematics. For instance two times two equals four. Also addition is for increment as one plus one equals two; three plus three equals six and so on and so forth. That is the energy of calculation through increment with multiplication and addition formulas. Manipulations, drawings, arts and everything put together are from **THE FATHER GOD** and they all materialize the Glory of **THE FATHER GOD**. Add them all together and that equals **THE FATHER GOD**.

Addition is **THE FATHER** and **MOTHER** and '**On**', is equal to **HE** is the **Son** and that becomes plural. When one is added to another one that addition energy will bring **On** as the equal to and the answer is the **Son** as **On**, *Eno*. These are what you must learn and **UNDERSTAND** today as the

"Abasi Mu-Udim" The Creator and Creations

PHENOMENAL ENTITY OF THE FATHER GOD, THE BLESSED MOTHER and the celebration.

That is why **I** advised the whole world, Africa, Akpan, Adiagha and **MOTHERS** as the **MU-UDIM** of **THE FATHER GOD** to celebrate **THE SUPREME WORD**.

There is the Glorification of **MU-UDIM**

And there is the Glorification of **THE FATHER** that is, **ALPHA**, as alone and the Glorification of **MOTHER AND FATHER** as **OMEGA, THE A** to **Z. THE FATHER AND THE MOTHER** only, form **OMEGA**. **THE FATHER GOD** alone is **ALPHA** and when the **Son** that is **Eno**, is involved then the Glory of **THE FATHER GOD** and **THE MOTHER GOD** is revealed. And that is today is a wonderful day, because of this wonderful Lecture Revelation for all **WOMANHOOD** to understand that their problems are solved from today. That is, if you believe and have patience. Every woman should have a copy of this Lecture Revelation. Even your child should know this. You should teach your child this lesson. Let your child know that premature **on** will bring disaster. Teach your child that when the mother and the father come together and **on** themselves, what will come out is a child, whether you believe it or not. Don't allow anything to be overdue because if you do, what happened between Lucifer and **THE FATHER GOD** will happen to you therefore always allow **COMPROMISE, FLEXIBILITY, UNDERSTANDING** and **TRUTH** to reign in the family. Do not pretend your child does not know about the business of men and women in this capacity. As soon as she experiences menstruation she will know even she may be innocent. Nonetheless, **NATURE** is very close these days therefore most children know these things even from inside their mother's wombs.

A child inside the womb knows this before birth. They have the instinct therefore be very; very careful because when they embark on premature '**On**' then problems arise from there. And that is what leads to abortion, which is killing. And from there, the roam about souls start haunting them. And their star is spoilt and that is where all their problems will come from. If you have that problem, it is very hard to solve it.

From today, the glory of **WOMANHOOD** has returned fully to all women. They **UNDERSTAND** themselves that they should have patience and humility. They should understand that they should learn the lessons of this Lecture Revelation and allow things to mature before they '**On**' them because if they **On** prematurely, then problems start from there.

CONCLUSION B: ABASI MU-UDIM THE MOTHER GOD OF CREATION THE MULTIPLE SELF

I have already said the above in this Lecture Revelation. I have explained that **GOD THE FATHER** became **MU-UDIM** when **HE** manifested as **THE MOTHER GOD** with the Womb of Nature to come out with all multiples of creations and beauty which is **GOD**. Everything on earth motivated via The Spoken Word is **GOD**. That is the phenomenon that makes things to be **On** because without that phenomenon, everywhere would be empty. Everywhere would be silent. Everywhere would be darkness therefore; **THE SUPREME WORD** seasonal celebration is a **MUST** for every soul.

If you really want the blessing in your family and you want to partake of the life in *THE SUPREME FUTURE* and to attract everything good to your life, then do not ignore the program called *THE UNIVERSAL SUPREME WORD SEASON CELEBRATION*, which is from First of October to the Tenth of October of every year, which is also, The Glorification of **GOD OF MU-UDIM** and **KIET-A-KIET ABASI**. When you do this then all is well with you. Nigeria, Africa, and the whole world should celebrate during that period. It is the celebration of **GOD OF MU-UDIM**, as the **GLORIFICATION** of **GOD OF MU-UDIM** and also the **GLORIFICATION** of **AKPAN** that is, **ALPHA, KIET-A-KIET ABASI**, the representative of **KIET-A-KIET ABASI, ALPHA** and the representative of **GOD OF MU-UDIM, THE MOTHER GOD** on earth, **THE GOD OF PLENTIFUL**, and **THE GOD OF MULTITUDE** and **THE PLURAL GOD** which is **LOVE**. With Love **WE On** and had the **Son, The Utinidem, Eno idem, Eno Abasi. Eno** is **On**. This is the meaning of the **Son**, but the son is actually the twisting of tongue changed *Eno* to **Son**.

CONCLUSION C: **I AM THE FATHER GOD IN TOTAL CONTROL**

I AM THE FATHER GOD therefore **I AM** in total control of everything and that is why **I** decoded this Lecture Revelation. Since **I** decoded this Lecture Revelation for **PEACE**,

LOVE, HUMILITY, ONENESS, COOPERATION, KINDNESS, and **PATIENCE** and for all good things, it has energy of all these things.

Multiply the **SELF OF THE FATHER GOD** in you for you to represent **THE FATHER GOD ALMIGHTY** in a proper way. When you have this **WORD** in you, you become '**GOD PRESENT**' and you are blessed.

All the people that WORK under this WORD, PROMOTE this **WORD**, TRANSCRIBE this **WORD** and help to PRODUCE this **WORD** are all blessed. You are blessed women for **THE BLESSED MOTHER MU-UDIM**. You are contributing a part to make everybody to become one by helping to publicize this **WORD** by making this **WORD** available to all. That is why **ETE** ROYAL UNIVERSAL FAMILY is well blessed because those who promote this record and help the world to improve by helping the world to move away from darkness to **LIGHT** and Help every mind and all **WOMEN** are abundantly blessed.. **WOMEN** think they are the downfall of the world but it is not the women.

Today! The root of **WOMEN'S** problem is revealed therefore it is solved. Lack of information made women to misunderstand things. If you want a woman to hate you, hide some information from her. If you talk to a woman she can forget food because all women like chatting. They like you to tell them stories. They want you to inform them of things in advance even if it is something that is not true but if you just say it to a woman she will be satisfied with that.

If you don't talk to a woman you are in trouble. That was what happened during creation. **THE FATHER GOD'S Object Soul** did not speak because of being busy with creations and all the manifestations on earth. That made Lucifer furious because she did not **UNDERSTAND** so she rebelled with the other selves of **THE FATHER GOD**. She took them and rebelled. Nonetheless, today! That problem is solved. That is why if you don't think evil there is no evil. If you don't speak evil there is no evil. If you don't practice evil there is no evil. Humanity is the cause of everything, which is **On**.

If you don't '**On**' nothing will happen. That is, if you don't speak nothing is happening and that is what is going on now. The current of electricity is always there but if you don't switch it on, it won't be on. **I AND MY FATHER ARE ONE** is **I AND MY FATHER ARE ON**. That is the **SON**, the **ON** therefore, **I** use this opportunity to bless the entire womanhood.

THE ABASI MU-UDIM, THE MOTHER GOD has blessed all **WOMEN. MOTHER** means **MU-UDIM, ABASI MU-UDIM. FATHER** means **KIET-A-KIET ABASI**. Only one **GOD, THE FATHER GOD** exists.

So, today! You have understood that **KIET-A-KIET ABASI** projected **HIMSELF** to **MU-UDIM** and had **ON**, which is **THE SPOKEN WORD, THE SON OF GOD** and everything is well on earth. **ENO ABASI** and **ENO ETE** for **THE BLESSED MOTHER, THE FATHER GOD** has blessed the entire world, in the name of Our Lord Jesus Christ, *Amein*.

THANK YOU FATHER

Part Three

OUR DIVINE SELVES THE HOLY SPIRIT SECRET REVEALED

MU-UDIM

Part Three

OUR DIVINE SELVES THE HOLY SPIRIT SECRET REVEALED

In the name of Our Lord Jesus Christ
In the blood of Our Lord Jesus Christ
Now and forever more, *Amien*

Today! It pleases **ME THE FATHER GOD** to give this Lecture Revelation, which is Part Three of **MU-UDIM, THE BLESSED MOTHER GOD**. The title of Part Three is **OUR DIVINE SELVES, THE HOLY SPIRIT THE SECRET REVEALED**. Or **THE HOLY SPIRIT, DIVINE SELF OF THE FATHER GOD, THE SECRET IS NOW REVEALED**. This Lecture Revelation of today is about the events that would have happened in the original system. **I** gave a similar Lecture Revelation titled: ***THE WORLD THAT WAS TO BE: WINDOS & WINIADOS*** in which **I** tried to bring out the information about the perfect system that was interrupted. That Lecture Revelation has been transcribed but not yet published. It was titled, **THE WORLD THAT WAS TO BE.** It was about ***Windos And Winiados, The Locus Parents* -The Blessed Earth With The Perfect System**. What **I AM** now doing to establish the perfect system of the world is that instead of starting from up downwards, **I** started from down and come upwards. The interruption of the system by the intruder turned the system upside down. And that was all because of misunderstanding.

THE SECRET REVEALED OUR DIVINE SELF THE HOLY SPIRIT is when **MU-UDIM** was being a busybody by not exercising patience thereby started breeding because she wanted children. Then the problem started with her reaction of not having things immediately as she wanted. And that problem caused death to exist. It was after the existence of death that **OUR DIVINE SELF** now came to be. The other self is still not giving up. People chant Satan, Satan and Satan! You sit down there bothering yourself with Satan but what about **THE HOLY SPIRIT**? You see that? **I** will make the whole world to know something today.

Adam was natural and as that natural was not perfect, it gave chance to the spiritual which is perfection. Without death, without that problem, without sin, which established death, how would the spiritual come to be established? The spiritual would not have established if there was no death, since the creation had already started because the first **On** had already been on. It is a wonderful secret and a wonderful mystery that took place.

As **I** explained before, when the grain of a corn has not died, it cannot bring out a new life that is, new seeds. When the fruit or seed of any plant is not dead, it cannot germinate to bring out its new life or new fruits. So, it is like that. Summer brings winter and winter brings summer and the mild weather in-between the two. Death brings life. Life brings death but the problem that humankind faced was that there was lack of understanding. You can see a good thing now but since you do not know that thing, you would throw it away and probably call it a bad thing. For instance, when Princess Mfon Etteh was sick in Manchester and then brought to Liverpool it was not actually sickness. She was not ill but **THE FATHER GOD** was working on her, changing her and preparing her for this job.

During that renovation, **I** kept three skips to put the building raw materials, some left over stuff, waste disposal and all sorts of things. At some point at the early months of her condition, **I** sent angels to go and give her some tablets and injections. She refused the medication **I** instructed to be administered on her. She refused and said that she does not take medicine. The illness that would have taken a few weeks to finish now took longer time. She did not have the Higherself to know that the medicine was spiritual and that what she was experiencing was a dream. Suppose it is now, maybe she would understand that this is **THE FATHER GOD'S** business.

It is like in the physical, when your spirit has not grown, you can miss millions of good things when you are presented with good things spiritually, you would term it to be a bad thing. For instance, if HRM King Solomon David Jesse **ETE** did not have a Higherself that is, if He had not come to this world seven times and become higher in spirit now, then when he saw how **I** preserved His soul, He would have thought He was going to die. He had a dream and saw that **I** had put Him inside a big coffin which was in the form of an altar. It looked like an altar but had the shape of a big coffin, laid with a red carpet. He was inside there, Him and **I, THE FATHER GOD**. When He woke up He understood and did not panic because **I** told

"Abasi Mu-Udim" The Creator and Creations

Him that that was where **I** hid His soul, Him and **ME**. If He did not know He would have started lamenting that He was in a coffin and that He was going to die. He could have even fasted to take that protection away.

When you do not understand anything you can spoil a lot of things. **I** show good things to a lot people in spirit but because sometimes the spirit presents things differently, they would come back and start crying that they saw bad things so **I** have now changed the gear. You must go to school first before **I** employ you. That means you must understand things first. Previously **I** employ people and train them while they work. The training at work caused **ME** a lot of hell. So, now don't work! **I** will give you food to eat. Go for training first. When you have finished training then come and work so that **MY** work would be professionally done. **Enye! Odudu!**

So, not having the higherself then caused Princess Mfon Etteh many years of problems? She was still given the spiritual tablets and injections eventually, at another time in a different way as she missed the ones of day. So, in due course she took the spiritual medication that she refused at previous times. They were spiritual tablets and medications and she said no that she does not take mundane medication. She equated the spiritual tablets and injections with the physical drugs that have all the side effects and cause other adverse effects when taken. She later started looking for the spiritual medicines.

*"I didn't understand **FATHER**!"*

Of course you did not understand. That is what **I AM** talking about. The premature stage of life causes problems to mankind. And how many people want to learn? Now **I** have come down by **MYSELF** to give all these Lecture Revelations. Even for you people that are recording, writing and transcribing these Lectures Revelations, how many have you learned? You believe that you are the cooks and so you have lots of food. But if you are not careful you will go home hungry. That is what happens sometimes. Those who cook the food fill full already. By the time they discover that they have not really eaten, sometimes most of the food is gone and they find that they are hungry. As for **ME I** cook and eat o! **I AM** cooking and eating as **I** go along. Ask those cooks what they eat as they cook.

Anyone that works in the minting house and say they do not see money, *na lie – o!* They do lots of business! If **I** tell you how much money the minting people steal, you will wonder. They even take the raw papers to go and develop at their homes. I know all these secrets. The reason **I AM** saying this is because **THE DIVINE SELF OF THE HOLY SPIRIT HAS REVEALED THE SECRET NOW**.

When the time of something is not due and you force yourself to do that thing you are in trouble.

A: **WHEN THE WORD BECAME MAN AND DIED**

You see that! This is now the secret. **I AM** bringing out a secret now. All the problems of Lucifer about misunderstanding and lack of patience were because nothing was working then until afterwards. It was all because **I** exposed the **WORD**. I took the **WORD** to go and put in man.

Lucifer who was the physical representative of the Spirit could not operate without **ME**. What then could she do then about having children? She was a **Mother.** She represented **ABASI MU-UDIM. I** was busy transferring those souls to materialize in the world. She had to wait! She was to wait until **I** finished what **I** was doing. Since she could not wait she came back and caused all the problems.

Lucifer wanted to bring out children by herself. She wanted to switch **On** by herself to have children but she did not have fuel to generate enough electricity current, so death occurred. That was why the instruction: Thou shalt not eat that fruit because when you eat ye shalt die. What is death? Death is a temporary situation. That is when the electricity is off and when it is off, then that is it.

That fruit in the Garden of Eden that they were asked not to eat but ate, consumed the energy of the small battery they had and so the current as the energy finished and there was no more energy.

The sexual organs of a woman and man are the generating points of energy of life in the physical reality. Human beings, both men and women can stay alive for a very long time if they don't have too much sexual activity. This is especially so for men. They can live longer if they refrain from too much indulgence in sexual acts because the more the man indulges in the act, the lesser his life span. This is doubly so when a man indulges in self-manipulation to expel this energy of life in him. It is a one-sided act and so a waste of energy. There is no return of energy. If Adam had lived for up to one thousand years, he would have lived forever. If he had lived the few years left of his life to complete one thousand years, he would have lived forever. He wouldn't die again. Adam lived for nine hundred and thirty years.

After Adam made that mistake **I** took him and kept him on top of the mountain for fasting for forty days which **I** declared for him. Do you think that forty days was actually forty days? Do you know how many years **I** called forty days? Never mind that one.

So, Eve sat down here while Adam was there on top of the mountain. People erroneously believe that Lucifer was a man. Supposing she was a man, he would have gone to sleep with Eve and had a way with her, because she was alone whilst Adam was on the mountain. She cried and cried and cried. She cried and cried and cried some more because Adam was, very, very far. So, so out of reach. At some point Adam could not bear her cries again and so he threw himself down from the mountain and his body broke into pieces. It was that blood of Adam when Adam killed himself as he fell from the mountain because of Eve that made **ME** to promise that **I** would save mankind. And who

"Abasi Mu-Udim" The Creator and Creations

caused that mountain to be there? Ha! It is not Satan. You must know.

When he was tempted by Satan and Adam fell, **I** puffed up the sand by making the noise *woooohhh!* The land that was plain became a mountain and Adam could not come down from there so He stayed there! He did not and could not see Eve for a very long time so Eve cried and cried and cried. Then Adam fell down from the mountain and crashed on the ground *craaahmmm!* And was in pieces. **I** said that is a lie! You are not dying anything! So, **I** put him back together. When **I** saw that blood on the ground **I** could not stand it. So, **I** said to Adam, Sorry! In five and half days **I** will send **The WORD** to come and redeem you. That is, his own Higherself. And would The **WORD** come to redeem Adam? Adam had to die physically before he could resurrect again. It was five thousand and five hundred years before the **WORD** who is Christ came. Was that five and half days? **I** said one thousand years is like one day in the sight of the **LORD**. That was what happened.

It was five thousand and five hundred years before **THE WORD**, the Higherself, the actual **WORD** that was living in Adam, could take an assumed body of Adam to come back. And that was the Second Adam who was **SPIRITUAL**. What caused that? It is the phenomenon of life and death.

What was the death? It was the body of Adam. And what was the life? It was the Spirit of Adam. The Spirit came to live again on earth, born through the dead body of Eve as **MU-UDIM**. Eve became the mother called The Blessed Virgin Mary, **THE BLESSED MOTHER** who is referred to by some as **THE BLESSED MOTHER**, "pray for us." This is why **I** revealed this information in this Lecture Revelation of today.

So, today! You must understand that **I** have what is called **THE HOLY SPIRIT, THE HOLY MOTHER** and that is **ABASI MU-UDIM**, the **NATURE**. It is no more a carnal situation because it has become spiritual. As natural Adam became spiritual Adam, Eve must also become a spiritual **MOTHER** and that is the reason for **THE TRINITY, THE HOLY SPIRIT OF TRUTH, THE COMFORTER and HE** is both **female** and **male**, as it was in the beginning. With this, the problem of humankind is solved for eternity.

If you are not in spirit and have humility and with the **HOLY SPIRIT**, you will not be able understand this Lecture Revelation. You will call it mystic. Which mystic person can talk like this? Nonetheless, **THE FATHER GOD HIMSELF** is a mysterious **GOD**.

This is the Lecture Revelation of **THE FATHER GOD**. So, if you can think well, speak well and have love and humble yourself then, everything can become clear in your head, in your brain and in your heart because this is the Spirit of Wisdom, the Wide Angle of **THE FATHER GOD**, for the nearer people of **THE FATHER GOD**.

Christ came and because of that the **HOLY SPIRIT** is able to live in human beings again and become **GOD PRESENT** to teach humankind everything by exposing all the information in **THE SPIRITUAL LIBRARY OF THE FATHER GOD** so that humankind would help their soul.

So you see, it was five thousand five hundred years, which was the five and a half days that the **WORD** became flesh and dwelt among men as **THE KING OF KINGS AND THE LORD OF LORDS**. When that **WORD** died everything became well and that is why when it is said that **THE WORD BECAME MAN AND DIED** it means when everything became well.

When I revealed this in the Lecture Revelation titled, ***THE WORLD THAT WAS TO BE: WINDOS, WINIADOS AND WINIADOSA*** I spoke in a different tone from how I speak here. I decoded the original tongue in this one because of **MU-UDIM, THE BLESSED MOTHER.**

MOTHER – MU-UDIM
FATHER – ALPHA, ALONE,
ABASI KIET-A-KIET AND
ABASI MU-UDIM.

The other one is **ABASI KIET-A-KIET**, which means **SINGULAR GOD** but this one is **ABASI MU-UDIM** and that is **GOD OF MULTITUDE, GOD OF PLENTY**, and **GOD OF LOVE**. It is NOT **GOD OF LOVE** of fornication. But **GOD OF LOVE – LOVE ONE ANOTHER. GOD** of Admiration, Goodness, Joyousness, Happiness, Forgiveness, Oneness, Mercifulness… and more and that is the **LOVE I AM** talking about therefore w**hen The Word Became Man And Died** everything became well because the price of the penalty of that oxymoron incident was paid. And Adam became renovated. The human body became renovated and conducive for **THE FATHER GOD** to live in again.

B: **THE PROJECTION OF MY HOLY SELF**

When the **SPOKEN WORD** became man and died, **WE** now came back. This means that the house that was polluted has become clean and secured. **MY** Divine Self, **THE HOLY SPIRIT** now came back to humankind and produced a **PROJECTION OF THE HOLY SELF**. That is what is called **THE HOLY SPIRIT**.

THE HOLY SPIRIT is different from **Holy Ghost**. **The Holy Ghost** is the Holy Son of God while **THE HOLY SPIRIT** consists of **THE FATHER GOD** and **THE MOTHER GOD**. And you have to understand these things to prevent you from misunderstanding things. Don't forget! Don't forget the important things.

Remember that when Jesus Christ was baptized The Dove of **GOD** revealed HIM. Don't forget that before **CHRIST** was born, **THE HOLY SPIRIT** was HIS **FATHER**. HE was conceived by the power of **THE HOLY SPIRIT** therefore, *HE IS THE SPIRIT.* The Divine **SPIRIT, THE HOLY SPIRIT** was always in existence and it was that same **HOLY SPIRIT** that passed through Adam and Eve to give birth to Abel therefore, when Abel died, he produced the **Force of the Holy Ghost**, as the first **Holy Ghost** in the land of souls. That became the Identification Spirit in the form of a **Dove** and that **Dove** represented the **Holy Ghost**. And that is why **The Holy Ghost** is different from **THE HOLY SPIRIT**. You have to understand that so that you don't get confused about **The Holy Ghost** and **THE HOLY SPIRIT**.

When **OUR LORD JESUS CHRIST** resurrected, it was **The Holy Ghost** that was talking. That was the inspiration as **THE FATHER GOD'S POSITIVE SELF** that took charge. All the negative people that die with their evil in them become vampire and witchcraft spirits souls. Abel became **The Holy Ghost** when he died because he was positive and was living a Godly life. All the positive people that die in a Godly manner are **Holy Ghost**. And all the negative people that die with their demonic ways are the witchcrafts spirits souls, evil ghosts, demons and bad ghosts. These are the ones that inspire the soothsayers, native doctors, juju doctors and all those groups of practitioners. Where, **THE HOLY SPIRIT** and **The Holy Ghost** inspire all the prophets of **THE FATHER GOD**. For instance, if you are good and work for **THE FATHER GOD** and you die, when you come back your former spirit as the former you will inspire you and that means that you are with **The Holy Ghost** and **THE HOLY SPIRIT** Nonetheless, **THE HOLY SPIRIT HIMSELF** is **I THE FATHER GOD** called **THE TRINITY GOD, THE SPIRIT OF TRUTH** that has never visited this world until this time as **I AM** now physically here because the death of **CHRIST** made it possible. And thereafter, **THE FATHER GOD AND THE MOTHER GOD**, the Divine Selves met together to produce the last **PERSONIFIED WORD** called **THE HOLY SPIRIT OF TRUTH** who came to bear witness for **THE TRUTH** about **THE SPOKEN WORD THE SUPREME WORD**, which is **OUR LORD JESUS CHRIST, THE FATHER GOD ALMIGHTY**. Therefore, **THE TRINITY GOD** is one in essence. **THE FATHER GOD** has never been three. **HE IS ONE** but works in diverse ways but as one entity.

    THE TRINITY GOD is in humankind. You are with the Trinity, the Physical Trinity and Spiritual Trinity. When you have the Holy Spirit, you are with the Spiritual Trinity. When you don't have the Holy Spirit you are still physical trinity. The **blood** and **water** and **spirit**

in you represent the Trinity **GOD**, which is the physical trinity in everyone. That is what you have to understand in this Lecture Revelation of today because **THE BLESSED MOTHER, THE ABASI MU-UDIM** is the fulfilment of **THE HOLY SPIRIT**. Now everything has become new and glorifies **THE FATHER GOD ALMIGHTY** through the Power of **THE HOLY SPIRIT**.

The NATURE of **THE FATHER GOD** and the WAYS of **THE FATHER GOD** is THE MORE YOU LOOK THE LESS YOU SEE. You can only take what you hear and believe and improve your soul than to say you will study **THE FATHER GOD**. If you study **THE ME FATHER GOD** you will NEVER know **THE FATHER GOD**. But when **THE FATHER GOD** wants you to know **ME, I** will reveal **MYSELF** to you. Just like what you are hearing now, if you eschew all manners of pomposity and take what you hear then, **THE HOLY SPIRIT** via this inspiration will help you to understand more.

From this you should now understand that **THE PROJECTION OF MY HOLY SELF** became possible after the death of **CHRIST**. The death of Christ was that, **THE SUPREME WORD OF THE UNIVERSE** killed the physical body. That is, **HE** killed the carnal part of the **MOTHER** that confused the system that is, the flesh. Everything thereafter became a naked spirit. As a result, it became possible for **THE HOLY SPIRIT** to come down physically to teach humankind all things therefore, you now hear **THE FATHER GOD** in a plain language and without ceremony.

People wondered how **GOD** would talk again. **THE FATHER GOD** even talks now more than before because previously **THE FATHER GOD** talks through angels. You have to do so many things before you hear the spirit talk, but today **I, THE FATHER GOD** talks directly in your heart.

And those who have sanctified themselves for **THE FATHER GOD** will see **ME** talking to them face to face. Just as **I AM** giving this Lecture Revelation now, **I AM** talking face to face. And all of you who are here hearing **ME** and seeing **ME** and listening to this **WORD ALL BLESSED**! And your sins have been forgiven you! And this **WORD** has cleaned you! And you live by this **WORD**. And all is well with you! No poverty! No problems! No hindrances for you! **THE BLESSED MOTHER** has blessed all of you and opened your way! Wonderful blessing! Wealth! You are healthy, wealthy living souls from today! Maximum protection! Maximum insurance! And maximum security! - For you all in the name and blood of our Lord Jesus Christ, *Amein*!

C: THE BIRTH OF THE HOLY SPIRIT COMFORTER ON EARTH

It is the projection of **MY HOLY SELF** that manifested The Physical Birth Of **THE HOLY SPIRIT** on Earth, just as **THE FATHER GOD On** in The Virgin Mary manifested the birth of **CHRIST**. Christ HIMSELF came on earth was called **ON**. That is the middleman, the energy, **THE SPOKEN WORD OF THE SPIRIT, THE SON OF GOD** who is as well and is called *Eno*.

When people here of 'The Birth of the Holy Spirit Comforter on Earth' they argue, ponder and ask whether **THE HOLY SPIRIT** can be given birth to. Why can **THE HOLY SPIRIT** not manifest through the process of birth? Every word spoken is given to birth. All the words everyone has uttered eventually manifest as human beings. Just like all these **FATHER'S TALK (GOD PRESENT)** Lecture Revelations you are hearing, they will all eventually come to be born as human beings one after another. As a matter of fact every sentence of them will possibly manifest as a human being. It depends what **I THE SUPREME NATURE** wants to do with them.

If **I** see that there is the possibility of a certain word or sentence becoming good then, **I** will help that word or sentence to materialize physically and properly on earth as a human being. Then that word that manifested is the one that will come to practice that word. Do you think you can practice the **WORD** of **GOD**? People have tried all sorts of things to practice the Word of God but cannot. The reason is that people speak evil words and eventually all those evil words manifest as human beings, including the person that spoke them and practice that evil they spoke. In that same factual reasoning, all the good words that **I AM** speaking now will materialize as human beings and come to practice these good words so if you refuse to practice these words, the words will practice themselves!

What did **I** say? **I** stipulate that seventy-two million Senior Christ Servants HRM King Solomon David Jesse **ETE** will multiply on earth. These ones will come because of this

FATHER'S TALK (GOD PRESENT) because **I THE FATHER GOD** will become these people. I will only use His house and since I will use His house as the harbour of KING SOLOMON SPIRITUAL LIBRARY, the same soul will multiply through these words, just as **OUR LORD JESUS CHRIST** came as the modified Adam as a spiritually modified Adam and HE became higher than the natural Adam. When this WORD will start to multiply you will see the Glory of **THE FATHER GOD** in full force on this earth, called **Combined Service of GOD as Combined, Combined, and Combined Forces Services of THE FATHER GOD** the Senior Christ Servants. And that is when everywhere will be **FATHER GOD! FATHER GOD! FATHER GOD!**

HRM King Solomon **ETE** will not take the glory of **THE FATHER GOD**. He will still remain the Senior Christ Servant of **THE FATHER GOD**. The title His Royal Majesty is the title **I** give to Him to superimpose all nonsense because it is **THE FATHER GOD** that is His Royal Majesty.

I AM His Father THE KING OF KINGS AND THE LORD OF LORDS.

If you think this WORD is not true go and speak your own and make it to be true because every word shall come to pass. If you say it is not **I THE FATHER GOD** that speaks these words then go and talk for **THE FATHER GOD** or go and talk for the **MOTHER** or for yourself and call it Myself Talk or Mother's Talk because this one is called **FATHER'S TALK (GOD PRESENT)**. So, when you go to talk your own, will call it Mother's Talk (Mother Present)? Or you want to call it Son Talk (Son Present)? Try and see whether it will yield anything. It is only **THE FATHER GOD** that knows the secret of **HIS** Kingdom. And it is only those who love one another that can accept this message. And when you accept this message all is well with you. **THE BLESSED MU-UDIM OF GOD OF ALL CREATIONS** called **THE BLESSED MOTHER** has blessed you and all is well with you. When you listen and accept the truth, then the truth has set you free, in the name and blood of Our Lord Jesus Christ, *Amein.*

D: AS IT WAS IN THE BEGINNING SO IT SHALL BE NOW AND FOREVER

Some people still argue that The Holy Spirit is not here. That The Holy Spirit has not yet come. So, *na* you come? (So, is it you that has come?) Or is it when **I** start talking and bearing record of **MYSELF** as **THE HOLY SPIRIT OF TRUTH** that you will heed? Who is supposed to bear **MY** record for **ME**?

You are all full of carnality, the whole world. Everybody is serving money. Everybody takes money as **GOD**. Some take women as **GOD**. Others take men as **GOD**. Everybody takes all sorts all sorts of mundane things as **GOD**. But what about **THE SUPREME WORD**, who cares about **HIM**? Yet you are using the **WORD**! Nobody takes the **WORD** as anything! Nobody even believes that **THE FATHER GOD** created Heaven and Earth and posterized **HIMSELF** by manifesting through **THE SUPREME WORD** and **THE WORD** manifested **HIMSELF** through humankind as **THE TRINITY GOD** on earth. Nobody takes notice of that.

'Oh you should not worship man. You should worship **GOD**' people say but where is the **GOD** that you must worship? You rather worship animals. Almost all countries of the world put birds, lions and other animals as their emblem, instead of putting human beings as their emblem. At least now Britain has tried now with their money because they have put their Queen and some of their notable people on their money however in the past, they used to put animals! Animals are still on their emblem and even on their Queen's insignia. **I AM** telling them to remove those animals that you have put there! **I** repeat remove those animals from your insignias and replace them with human beings that **I THE SUPREME WORD** lives in! Because human beings are the image and the **WORD** is the likeness of **THE FATHER GOD** in humankind.

If you knock your head on the ground for a human being, you are not doing that for that person per se. You are knocking your head on the ground for **THE WORD** that lives in that person. And that person in turn will knock their head on the ground for you. He or she is not doing that for you but for **THE WORD** in you. **HE IS THE SPIRIT** is within you. The force within you is the force of life and that life itself is **THE SPOKEN WORD** that makes you to speak. When that force goes out of you, you will drop dead and that means that you are finished! You become garbage. Yet you do not respect **THE WORD**.

You don't respect **THE WORD** at all because you ask, "Why am I going to celebrate **THE WORD**?" Is it not the **WORD** that lives in your husband, your wife, your child, your father and your mother? It is the **WORD** and that is why when you celebrate **THE WORD** it means that indirectly you love everybody. You would not kill anybody again. You would not hate anybody again because you partaking in blessing. You are partaking in respect. And you are promoted by partaking with the celebration of ***THE UNIVERSAL SUPREME WORD SEASON CELEBRATION***. You are celebrating **THE FATHER, SON AND THE HOLY SPIRIT** in so doing. Through the celebration all is well with humankind for eternity because, **As It Was In The Beginning, So It Shall Be Now And Forever**, where **THE HOLY SPIRIT** teaches humanity everything because this was how **I** was talking to Adam. He named everything accordingly such as Goat, Chicken, Fish, Tree, Bird, and so forth because he was with **THE FATHER GOD. I** was talking to Adam in full swing just as **I AM** talking now, openly and plainly.

Adam was **GOD THE FATHER** on earth while **THE FATHER GOD** was talking through Adam as **GOD PRESENT** but when the Busybody Self came and spoilt things that did not happen again. Now it has happened again this time as it was that time so, it is World without End!

World without End is **WORD WITHOUT END, I THE SUPREME WORD THE CREATOR OF THE UNIVERSE** thanks **THE FATHER GOD ALMIGHTY** for not destroying humankind because of the love of **HIM, THE SPOKEN WORD**. Now **THE HOLY SPIRIT OF TRUTH** has now engineered humankind back for **HIMSELF** and mankind's problems are solved forever therefore, **THE BLESSED MOTHER** is **ABASI MU-UDIM** that has blessed the entire world because **SHE** is part of **ME** called **THE HOLY MOTHER**.

THE HOLY MOTHER'S glorification is as it is because **THE HOLY MOTHER** is the part of **MYSELF**. **SHE** is the **SELF** of **MYSELF** called **Add On**.

Add On brought out **On** and **Add Self, Adian, adian kiet.** *Adian adiagha, adian Akpan, adian udoh* and so on, that is it.

E: **THE FATHER GOD AND THE MOTHER GOD IS TO BRING BACK THE FIRST WORD PERSONIFIED**

Before the **WORD** came and became man and died and solved the problem of death, there was death that when you die you cannot resurrect. But now, that type of death has no power over the positive children of **THE FATHER GOD**. You can die now and resurrect in seventy-two hours that is, three days and three nights and you will take another body and come and serve **THE FATHER GOD** therefore, death is no longer a problem. There is no death for the positive children of **GOD** because **ABASI MU-UDIM** is at standby to bring you back on earth.

ABASI MU-UDIM is **THE BLESSED MOTHER GOD. AND THE FATHER GOD, KIET-A-KIET** is **THE WORD. I AM** the **LIGHT** that gives you everlasting life, the energy that you cannot die for eternity. **NO DEATH!** And that is why when you see a person of **GOD** and decide to go and kill him or her, you should know that killing him or her does not pose any harm to them. If you can kill the person that means you are favouring **ME,** but if you cannot kill that means that person's assignment is not finished. **THERE IS NO DEATH THEREFORE NO CHILD OF GOD SHOULD BE AFRAID OF DEATH ANYMORE**! You cannot die! Nobody can kill you!

If anybody wants to kill you, such a person will not be born on this earth. Even their mother

"Abasi Mu-Udim" The Creator and Creations

will not be pregnant with them. It will never happen at all! How would such a person be inside the woman to be born on earth? **I AM THE ONLY ADAUSUNG! (IN CHARGE) AND I DAUSUNG EVERYWHERE!**

Don't you see, **ADAUSUNG** means **ADD**, so, where will she subtract '**add**' and add without **ME**? **I AM THE ONLY ADD**. Before you add **ME** together to get **ON** you **MUST** pass through **ME**. **ON** is approval. Where will you get the approval for death or life without **THE FATHER GOD**? So, relax! Speak the truth! Do **THE FATHER GOD'S** work. If anybody could have been killed, it is HRM King Solomon David Jesse **ETE**. He would not have been alive for you to witness this **WORD**. None of you here would have been alive today for this. Even all of you have died and come back. HRM Queen Disem Solomon **ETE** died and came back. She was killed when she was a baby but because of her destiny to witness this **WORD I** kept her alive. As for HRM Majesty King Solomon David **ETE**, how many times have they killed Him? But because of His assignment to witness this **WORD, I** always returned Him alive. Not to mention Princess Mfon Etteh, hers is life topic. She has died and came back. **I** returned her to life to witness this

WORD. So, all of you have witnessed **THE EVERLASTING TESTIMONY OF EVERLASTING GOSPEL, THE HOLY SPIRIT OF TRUTH** and you have witnessed **THE ABASI MU-UDIM, THE BLESSED MOTHER** blessing **THE BLESSED WOMEN**. And the women in turn bless the whole world. This is the time for peace. This is the time for everlasting wealth. So, all is well with all positive children of **GOD** and all women today and their spirits are elevated in the name of Our Lord Jesus Christ, *Amien*.

THE FATHER GOD and **THE MOTHER GOD** brought **THE PERSONIFIED WORD** back on earth. That is why you see the final Adam here on earth. **HE** is **THE KING OF KINGS AND THE LORD OF LORDS** with **THE BLESSED MOTHER**. There is no confusion because everything is well organized. **I** have established that. You have **THE BLESSED FATHER**.

You have **THE BLESSED MOTHER**.
You have **THE NEW HEAVEN**
You have **THE NEW EARTH**
THE FATHER AND THE MOTHER made the **NEW HEAVEN AND THE NEW EARTH**. Now the journey has started! It is now a perfect journey and a perfect home, from

source to **destination** and from **destination** to **source.** So, those who are going to see *THE SUPREME FUTURE* and enjoy *THE SUPREME FUTURE* are those who practice **LOVE ONE ANOTHER**, oneness, equality, mercy, kindness, honesty, respect and those who do not plan any evil against someone and do not involve in killing of any kind.

Don't get involved with any killing. If you have committed abortion and apologized, then **THE FATHER GOD** has used the blood of Abel to forgive you, through the blood of **CHRIST**. If you do not practice forgive one another then that is your business. But no child of **THE FATHER GOD** should commit abortion. Abortion is murder! No children of **THE FATHER GOD** should kill or have anything to do with life extinction. If you preserve life and forgive one another, then you have the license to enjoy *THE SUPREME FUTURE* in the name and blood of Our Lord Jesus Christ, *Amien*.

Don't worry or be intimidated by those human beings that look huge, gigantic and menacing that are animals that have ganged up and seized everything in the whole world today. They are going to wax away. They will melt like the fresh flower you see in the morning and in the evening it wilts and melts away. And when these evil human animals go, that is final. They will never come back in this world again. Many thousands and millions of human beings that control this world in a bad way will never smell this world again. If they happen to come back they are coming to serve you, the positive children of **THE FATHER GOD**, whether they believe it or not.

All the people that want to have good positions in *THE SUPREME FUTURE* should become servants now. They should **LOVE ONE ANOTHER** and **APPRECIATE THE FATHER GOD** by partaking in *THE UNIVERSAL SUPREME WORD SEASON CELEBRATION*. It is **THE WORD** that is going to engineer your life.

If you would not accept this **WORD** therefore would not believe the **TRUTH** thereby failing to project the **TRUTH** and refuse to promote the **TRUTH** and would not celebrate the **TRUTH** as **THE SUPREME WORD** then you are grievously harming yourself because you cannot go on in life without **THE WORD**. There are no two ways about it. You cannot escape **HIM**. **HE** is **ADAUSUNG** in Heaven, on earth, in the Spirit

"Abasi Mu-Udim" The Creator and Creations

and Hades; everywhere, here and there, **HE IS THE WORD** therefore **HE IS THE LEADER**.

F: **ALL WOMEN ARE BLESSED, BLESSED MOTHER BLESSED WOMEN!**

> **WOMEN O - ON...** *TOP!*
> **WOMEN O -ON...** *TOP!*
> **WOMEN O -ON...** *TOP!*

WOMEN are all blessed! They will give birth to good children. They will have good names. I have joined positive names to positive women and they will have positive children. And women will not betray men. And men will not hate their wives. Everything is well. From today, women will not have busybody. They will have patience for things because **THE FATHER GOD** plans things in time. They will not go to meet any man when it is not yet time to do so. They will not complain that exercise of nature is overdue. They should not say that again. They should wait for the right time before they go for exercise of nature so that everything should work well. And **THE FATHER GOD** has helped young women not to go and do exercise of nature when the time is not yet right and result in them producing premature children. They should not **On** when they are not supposed to be **On**. They should allow **THE FATHER GOD** to **On** for them so that they would have good children. All is well in the name of Our Lord Jesus Christ, *Amien*.

G: THE HEAVEN AND THE NEW EARTH ARE BY THE PERSONIFIED HOLY SPIRIT, THE FATHER GOD THE NATURE SELVES BOTH NATURAL AND SPIRITUAL

Now, that **I, THE FATHER GOD ALMIGHTY**, have manifested as **THE PERSONIFIED HOLY SPIRIT OF TRUTH**, everything is well. Both **SPIRITUAL** and **NATURAL** nature are both fine now. All **I** want from humankind is humility, oneness, peace, love and to think and speak good words. Everyone should think well, speak well, see well, hear well and do well. When you do that you have no problem.

When your conscience asks you to do a bad thing, just pronounce, **GOD FORBID BAD THING!** As soon as you say that, that spirit will be shamed and would go away. Even if it comes one hundred times always say **GOD FORBID BAD THING!** If you read the Lecture Revelation titled ***PROGRESSING MIND*** you will see that. Advance your mind from all the rubbish and always think about good things so that all will be well with you, in the name of Our Lord Jesus Christ. Amen!

CONCLUSION A: **THAT IS WHY EVERYTHING HAS CHANGED FOR GOOD**

As a result of these pronouncements and ***THE GREAT UNIVERSAL CHANGE,* THE HOLY SPIRIT PERSONIFIED** has changed everything. I have modified the world, which includes the way human beings think, speak and interact with one another.

In the time past they thought that the spirit of witchcraft, the evil spirit, the spirit of bad things would take over the world. Now the story has changed. It is **THE HOLY SPIRIT THAT CONTROLS THE WORLD NOW** including the governments of everywhere in the world. Go to Great Britain you will see the new arrangements of things in their government and in their Monarchy. **THE HOLY SPIRIT** has taken control. Go to America **THE HOLY SPIRIT** has taken control. You can see the effect of ***THE GREAT UNIVERSAL CHANGE*** that has swept through America. Go

"Abasi Mu-Udim" The Creator and Creations

to Asia to places such as India, China and see the changes for good taking place. Go to the continent of Africa, all Africans have changed for good. It is the same thing in Israel and Palestine and all over the countries of the whole world. **THE FATHER GOD** has taken over the government of the whole world. **THE HOLY SPIRIT** now directs all the Presidents of every country and all the Heads of States, all the Prime Ministers in countries that have that sort of government and all Kings and Queens. Even the armies of all the countries of the world no longer go to war. They are now going to learn some skills that will channel them to the activities of helping one another. Nobody likes to die again. You can hear the soldiers crying again and again that they don't want to die. That means **THE FATHER GOD** has changed the soldiers. People do not want to die again because everybody wants to live and enjoy this world. They want to enjoy the **GIFT** of **THE FATHER GOD,** the *Eno Abasi.* **THE FATHER GOD** has used **HIS Eno** to change the whole world.

WOMEN are all blessed because **WOMEN** are peace. **WOMEN** mean **ABASI MU-UDIM**. **WOMEN** have the nature of plenteousness. They increase things. When you don't have

WOMEN in your church for instance, your church cannot grow. When there are no **WOMEN** in any place there is no peace in that place and no beauty. Such a place would not be nice. Who will cook for you? Who will make things nice and beautify the whole place for you?

WOMEN mean peace and sugar.

WOMEN really make things work well.

WOMEN do not stand for destruction.

WOMEN do not stand for temptation.

WOMEN do not make anybody to fall away.

THE FATHER GOD has given **WOMEN PATIENCE** to believe what is true so that when you speak the truth they believe you.

WOMEN will now have the **PATIENCE** to wait for **GOD'S TIME** in their life because previously they did not wait for **GOD'S TIME**. They would just do their own thing and that caused problems. But today! **THE FATHER GOD HAS GIVEN WOMEN THE SPIRIT OF PATIENCE,** long, long **PATIENCE**. And women have seen the Glory of **THE FATHER GOD**, in the name of Our Lord Jesus Christ, *Amein!*

CONCLUSION B: **IN THE FATHER GOD ALL WOMEN ARE BLESSED**

All these blessings come from whom? They come from **ME THE FATHER GOD, THE SUPREME WORD OF THE UNIVERSE.** Since a woman gave birth to **CHRIST** and **CHRIST** saved the whole world, **WOMEN ARE BLESSED.** Since a woman brought **THE PERSONIFIED HOLY SPIRIT** on earth **WOMEN ARE BLESSED.** Since a woman brought the life **ADAM, THE FATHER OF THE ENTIRE MANKIND, THE UNIVERSAL SHRINE, THE KING OF KINGS AND THE LORD OF LORDS WOMEN** are glorified just as **THE FATHER GOD** is glorified. All these blessings come from **THE FATHER GOD ALMIGHTY** to all humankind. And that is the blessing you receive today.

This day of THE RECEPTION OF **THE BLESSED MOTHER** is **THE BLESSED MOTHER FOR ALL WOMEN** AND MEN ALL OVER THE WORLD.

CONCLUSION C: **THE BLESSED MU-UDIM IS NOW THE HOLY SPIRIT**

COMFORTER A PERSONALITY WITH THREE CAPACITIES

You see that? **THE BLESSED MU-UDIM IS NOW THE HOLY SPIRIT COMFORTER** that is, the personality with three capacities. When you read the Lecture Revelation titled, ***THE PERSONALITY WITH THREE CAPACITIES*** you will see that **THE FATHER, SON** AND **THE HOLY SPIRIT** is **ONE PERSON** called **OOO OLUMBA OLUMBA OBU, GOD OF HEAVEN**, and **GOD OF SPIRIT SOUL AND GOD OF THE EARTH**. That means the **Spirit**, the **Soul** and the **physical**. **OOO** also means the **Spirit**, the **Word** and **Man**. **Man** is **Obu** (dust). *Ofim, mbat ye ntong.*

When someone is buried and these words are said *ntong ke ntong, ntan ke ntan, obu ke obu* (ash to ash, sand to sand, dust to dust). Where is *ofum ke ofum* (air to air)? That one had already left the body.

Therefore, today **I** have made everybody to understand what **OBU** is. It is **DUST**. That is *mbat, ntong, ikpokidem* (clay, ash, skin).

Every single human being on earth is **OBU (DUST OF THE EARTH)**.

Every single human being on earth is **OLUMBA (SOUL OF THE SPOKEN WORD "THE LIFE")**.

That is, you are all **OLUMBA OBU** whether you believe it or not. However, the only thing is that **NO** human being is **THE SPIRIT**.

Nonetheless that **SPIRIT** lives in the first **"OLUMBA"**.

That **OLUMBA** lives in **OBU**. Then this **OBU** that harbors **THE SPIRIT** is now a human being on earth. If you like you take this information, if you don't like then leave it. This is **THE FINAL HOLY SPIRIT** ideology, the belief that can **NEVER** fade away because **IT IS AN UNCHANGEABLE TRUTH**.

OLUMBA OLUMBA OBU – THE SPIRIT lives in the **SOUL** and the **SOUL** lives in **MAN**.

THE SPIRIT manifested **THE SPOKEN WORD** and **THE SPOKEN WORD** manifested **MAN** (the human beings) that is, **OBU** therefore every human being is **OBU**. And every human being has a **SOUL OF OLUMBA** that is, the **WORD** in every single human being. And that **SPIRIT** that manifested **THE SPOKEN WORD that** lives in you. So, you are Trinity. **OLUMBA OLUMBA OBU**.

"Abasi Mu-Udim" The Creator and Creations

OLUMBA does not mean one thing. It is the **COMPLETION OF THE WHOLE** called **THE FATHER GOD ALMIGHTY** that turned to be man, which includes a woman, animal, fish and bird and everything else. Nevertheless, it is **THE MORE YOU LOOK THE LESS YOU SEE.**

This **WORD** is the **TRUTH**. When you believe it, you are fine, but if you do not believe the **TRUTH** then you are not fine. Let the blessing of all blessing follow all human beings on earth through **THE BLESSED MOTHER** today now and forever more. *Amein*!

LET MY PEACE AND BLESSING ABIDE WITH THE ENTIRE WORLD NOW AND FOREVER MORE, *AMEIN*!

THANK YOU*UU* FATHER!

Prayer by HRM Queen Disem Solomon David **ETE**

Let thanks and praises be given to the **FATHER GOD** in the name of **OUR LORD JESUS CHRIST**
Let thanks and praises be given to **THE FATHER GOD** in the blood of **OUR LORD JESUS CHRIST**
Let thanks and praises be given to **THE FATHER GOD** and **THE MOTHER GOD, THE ABASI MU-UDIM** now and forevermore, *Amien.*

HOLY, HOLY, HOLY FATHER GOD thank you for this Lecture Revelation that blesses all women and all man and indeed all creation on this day that the **ABASI- MU-UDIM** has blessed all **HER** children therefore, with the blessing of the **BLESSED MOTHER GOD** and **THE BLESSED FATHER GOD** all is well with all creation for eternity, now and forever more, *Amien.*

Let thanks and praises be given to the **FATHER GOD** in the name of **OUR LORD JESUS CHRIST**

Let thanks and praises be given to **THE FATHER GOD** in the blood of **OUR LORD JESUS CHRIST**

Let thanks and praises be given to **THE FATHER**, **THE SON** and **THE HOLY SPIRIT COMFORTER, THE ABASI MU-UDIM** now and forevermore, *Amien*.

THANK YOU FATHER

"Abasi Mu-Udim" The Creator and Creations

Chapter Two

ABASI MU-UDIM
THE CREATOR AN CREATIONS

PART ONE
"SPIRIT" THE FATHER GOD

FATHER'S TALK
(GOD PRESENT)

Christ Our Lord, Fifteenth Judas Iscariot, FATHER, Two Thousand and Eight (AE/OC/BOOH) Saturday, Fifteenth, March, Year Two Thousand and Eight (15/03/2008)

In the name of our Lord Jesus Christ

In the Blood of Our Lord Jesus Christ

Now and forever more

PART ONE
"SPIRIT" THE FATHER GOD

Today it pleases **ME, THE FATHER GOD THE CREATOR OF THE UNIVERSE** to bring this great Lecture Revelation titled, **THE CREATOR AND CREATIONS:** *SPIRITUAL, NATURAL, MUNDANE OR ARTIFICIAL*

INTRODUCTION

This Lecture Revelation is one of the Lectures that **I** brought out as a Supreme Information from **MY** Archive Records to help mankind because **I** love humankind.

I created man to be **MY** image and likeness and **I** suffered so much for man. The **WORD** as

Love endeavoured in all aspects and situations to save humankind and now, **I** know that mankind is saved through the name and the blood of our Lord Jesus Christ.

I want every human soul, whether you are a child, an adult, man, woman, husband or wife, Head of State, family and you name it, whatsoever you are, no matter the name or position, to throw away pomposity, arrogance, academia, wisdom, scientific achievements, philosophic tendencies, positions and all. Since the **WORD** is all and all, you must subject to the **WORD** that created you. Subject yourself to the Truth and to the Recondite Wisdom. The recondite Wisdom is the Wideness Self of **MYSELF** that will bring you closer to **ME** wherever you are, to save your soul and also the physical world in general. This is the Manual of Understanding.

This Lecture Revelation is the **MANUAL OF UNDERSTANDING** on how to interact with **GOD** and yourself and the whole world in general

A: WHAT IS SPIRIT AND SPIRITUAL?

What is **Spirit** and **Spiritual**? That is the question. **I** know when people come across this question some will answer that they already know what spirit is and what spiritual is. If you know something and you know something again, what is bad about that?

Don't you know that **I, THE FATHER GOD** means 'progressing'? So, since **I** passed one second, should **I** not pass one second again? And since **I** passed one minute do you think **I** have not passed one minute again? And since **I** passed one hour, have **I** not passed one hour again? And since **I** passed one day have **I** not passed one day again? And since **I** passed one week have **I** not passed another week again? And since **I** passed one month, have **I** not passed another month again? And since **I** passed one year, have **I** not passed one year again? And since **I AM** forever do **I** not belong to forever?

Have **I** said because **I AM** this, **I** cannot be that?

If **I AM** this and **I AM** that, then **I AM** everything!

What is wrong about being **ALL AND ALL**?

I believe that the fruits of all the children of **GOD** as the ones, who have the inspiration of **THE FATHER GOD**, should be truth, humility and peace. The reason people do not count this as important is because they do not have the Higherself to understand why it is important for them to have humility, for instance.

You do not understand why it is important to be humble. You do not understand why it is important to love.

You do not understand why it is important to practice equality and be in oneness.

It is important because these components are the acting behaviours. They are the instincts that form emotions in your system. When you are peaceful, you have calm nerves that make you take time to accept things and to know things before you come into a conclusion about them. When you have mercy, it makes you not to condemn things easily, because you do not know whether that thing you want to condemn is good or bad. When you have love, it makes you to accept things because love makes you accept things as they are. You must accept something first before you will know whether that thing is good or not good.

Everything about **ME, THE FATHER GOD** with all **MY** components makes you to be a well arranged human being that represents **GOD** in reality. When **I** talk about the **Likeness** and the **Image** of **GOD**, it means you should be a well arranged person in every capacity of life and in all angles.

You should understand the meaning of the Wideness Angle of **GOD**, which brings everybody near to **GOD**. The Wideness Angle of GOD is Wisdom while Nearness of **GOD** is Clever and Understanding, because through Wisdom, you will Understand and through Understanding you will become Clever. That is why you are close to yourself.

So, ***What Is Spirit And Spiritual***? This is what people know, but not all of it. **I**, The SPIRIT is the only one that can tell you a little bit of who **I AM**.

THE SPIRIT IS ALL AND ALL.
THE SPIRIT IS EXISTENCE – EXISTING.
THE SPIRIT IS THE BEING.
THE SPIRIT IS THE TOTALITY OF TOTALITIES.
THE SPIRIT IS FORM and
Through **THE FORM**, formation took place.

Through **THE BEING** everything began.

Through **EXIST** everything becomes Existing.

Through **AMEN**, everything became alleluia and Hosanna.

"Abasi Mu-Udim" The Creator and Creations

That is why the **SPIRIT** is unheard-able, unseen-able and untouchable. However, the **SPIRIT** becomes Heard-able. The Heard-able made seen-able and seen-able became touchable because when you see something, it is possible to touch it and when you hear something, you reason that you could possibly see what you heard. Therefore, when **I** made **MYSELF** heard-able, the interest and curiosity became greater to see what **I** heard? Can **I** not see what **I** heard, **I** asked **MYSELF**? And the curiosity spirit of **ME** made **MYSELF** as Heard-able become seen-able. Oh, **MY MYSELF**, **I** have now seen what **I** heard, **I** said, then, **I** said, can **I** not touch? Again, **MY** curiosity spirit became so inquisitive and was eager to touch and feel so, **I** made **MYSELF** touchable and that brought the creations. **THIS IS THE SPIRIT**.

People claim that they went to spiritual world. It is a lie. People also claim to have seen spirit. It is a lie! 'Oh I heard the spirit!' It is a lie. You did not hear any spirit. You did not see any spirit and you certainly did not touch any spirit. You definitely did not travel to any spiritual world. No human being knows it. Even Satan does not know where spiritual world is.

SPIRIT IS **MYSELF** ALONE.
I AM UNHEARD-ABLE

"Abasi Mu-Udim" The Creator and Creations

I AM UNSEEN-ABLE and
I AM UNTOUCHABLE.

So, if there is a place you can't hear, you can't see and you can't touch, how will you visit that place? How will you know that place? It is an unknown thing.

What you are about to hear now is where you can visit. Also what you heard now is what you can hear and what you hear is what you can touch. Other than the aforementioned ignore anything that is termed spirit.

When **I** became heard-able as **I** projected **MYSELF** to make **MYSELF** heard-able, it was then **I** formulated **MYSELF** and made objects known as **Soul Objects**. The first of the soul objects was the heard-able -sound, which became the **Word.** The **Word** then made creations that formed soul objects. The soul objects tried to formulate themselves to be touchable things through the Supreme Nature. The soul object then camera itself and it self-camera itself that is, it projected itself to become the nature that you see, which became man, and which became everything.

As you must have deduced from the above, the formation of creation was in two stages. The first is the Spoken Word and the second is the soul creation. Then the physical manifestation follows afterwards as the next step. And this is the point where nature takes snapshots of object souls by itself when Nature Camera to bring objects out to the physical.

However, the creation of man was quite different because **I** created man with **MY** own hands and **I** transferred **MYSELF** as the host of air – *jhiiiiiih* into man. And then **I** stayed inside man as the Holy Spirit. This Holy Spirit is different from The Life. When a human being commits sin, the Holy Spirit goes out of the person, but the influence of the Holy Spirit still generates The Life as The General Life similar to the general supply of electricity.

When you first want to start building a house, before you start to build the house, the first thing that you must take to the site is electricity current. You must lay cables and connect electricity current so that with that you can then connect water. These are the first things that you will need to effectively work with the materials for building.

At this stage, the building is yet to be erected, but the current of electricity and the water is in placc and then you will probably build a small hut to hang your cloths and store your instruments of work. And most of the things that will be there for the building project will be temporary but the electricity and the water pipes will not be so. When you finish building the house, it is the same connection of electricity that you will use to wire the whole house. And the same thing goes for the water supply in the new building. The house, the water and the current become the three things that will remain permanent in that new house.

Prior to **ME, THE FATHER GOD, THE CREATOR** creating man, **I** first created other things. The reason **I** first created other things was that 'he who laughs last laughs the best'. If **I** had created man first, man would be empty and without food. So, **I** created food and everything and when they were plentiful and everything was equally beautiful and is beautiful. **I** built the whole universe and created everything then, finally, **I** created man with **MY** hands and **I** put man in the egg of nature.

When **I** created man and put him in the egg of nature, **I** breathed **MYSELF** *jzeeeeeeehhh* as the breath of life into that egg of nature. Then **I** broke it *kpowaaah* and the egg hashed and **I** came out and called **MYSELF** Adam. I become **God The Father** while in **ME, I AM THE FATHER GOD**.

So, **MY Thought, MY Instinct**, **MY Real Self** are the components that I turned to be *owo* (human), Adam. Then I saw the creations and I gave names to all the creations and admired them. Nonetheless, I still existed in the Sole capacity of '**HE** IS THE SPIRIT' but I became touchable since I had become seen-able. And the process was, from heard-able, I came to be seen-able and then to touchable and that is what is called '**THE TRINITY**.' The Father, Son and the Holy Spirit are one which represents your name, your soul of life and your physical body. And it also represents the liquid product or the material product, the name of the product and the package of the product.

Have I made it clear to mankind, the way these things work? Will you say you had this type of knowledge previously? If you have it, I AM sure it was not this type of **WISDOM**. As I AM sitting down here in the middle part of the United Kingdom (UK) England, **I AM** manifesting this Lecture Revelation through HRM King Solomon **ETE** and this is the same way I sat with Adam in the middle of the Garden of Eden and manifested everything. I AM doing the same thing now to reveal this knowledge and this wisdom and it means new creations. It means **I AM** pouring out **MY** Spirit and changing things. This **Word** that **I AM** giving today and all **THE FATHER'S TALK (GOD PRESENT)** Lecture Revelations are what **I AM** using to put things new and put things right in the whole world.

What is Spirit and Spiritual? Spiritual means everything The SPIRIT is doing it handles it spiritually which is unseen-able, but you can see it here and eventually becomes touchable but can first be heard and that is the **Spirit-tual**. Then the Soul and the 'Spirit-tual' is one thing – from 'Spirit-tual' to 'Soul-tual' – whatsoever you call 'tual' is all the same 'tual'. This means that the **Spiritualism** and **Soulism** is the copy of **The Spirit**. That soul which is the copy of **The Spirit** is an object, just like the object that imagination forms in your brain or in your heart.

Imagination is the soul as the idea that you have inside you. It means you have it, but it is not yet created. **I** have created them all in THE SPIRIT of **MYSELF,** but since it has not yet become physical, it is **Spiritual**. From the SPIRIT to **Spiritual** and that is the Soul Object. And that is what the Spiritual World is. It is not the Spirit World.

The SPIRIT has no world.

The SPIRIT is a phenomenon of a singular of **HIMSELF**.

HE has no deputy.

HE has no second.

HE has nothing of nothing. As a matter of fact, **THE SPIRIT IS THE SPIRIT** but the **Spiritual** is the formation of objects. That is, the copy of the Spirit that became has become an object soul via The **Word** because the first **Spiritual** is the **Word.**

This **Spiritual** is where people manipulate things. Anybody that has access to the **Spiritual** can manipulate things but you do not have access to **THE SPIRIT**. You cannot have a dream of the spirit world but you can have a dream of the **Spiritual** world therefore what is the **Spiritual** world is not **THE SPIRIT** World.

I AM THE SPIRIT and **I** established the **Spiritual World** where **I** keep all souls and that is the Hades or Dream World. Soul World is the original name where everything comes from. The Soul World is the world of supreme imagination and things come from and then return there.

The world of imagination is two. The first is the abstract-abstract that the imagination causes which has not yet taken the object form but when it is eventually created, it takes the object of the shadow world, which forever can never be lost, but what is in the imagination can be lost.

If a thought occurs to you and you do not write it down, when you forget it, then it is lost. It goes back to the memory. But as soon as you write the thought down or describe your thought or idea then, you can always recall it from the memory any time because it has formed the object soul or the shadow of souls that will remind you of how what was in your imagination looked like.

As soon as you have created the figure out of the object physically, even if the thing is no more there in the shadow, you can take a photo or video or even an audio of your physical creation. And this means that the imagination of that thing still exists which is what you call the **Spiritual world**.

Everything that **The WORD** produces from THE SPIRIT is also produced into the **Spiritual** called the World of Souls or the Soul Object World which is the store from which **I** take things for creation because that is where **I** store **MY** ideas for creation. That is where **I** store everything and from there **I** take whatever **I** require to do physical manifestation. This

WORD you are hearing now is stored there and it is called the **Unlimited Memory of GOD** as the **Soul World of the Word** and this is endless in expatiation. However, since **I** have expatiated so far it will help you to improve your understanding and conscience unto a higher consciousness about **GOD**.

B: **THE FATHER AND THE FATHER GOD**

How do you understand **THE FATHER** and **THE FATHER GOD**? **I** said The SPIRIT is **THE FATHER** and **THE FATHER** is **THE WORD** and that means the OWNER.

If you say 'in the name of **THE FATHER** that means you are worshipping **ME** THE SPIRIT because you cannot say 'in the name of THE SPIRIT. You can only say **THE FATHER**. If you call **ME, THE FATHER** that means you have honoured **ME** as THE SPIRIT that owns everything.

What is **THE FATHER GOD?**
THE FATHER is raw material as a raw thing that needs refining.
THE FATHER means **Raw**.
SPIRIT means **Raw**.
How do you refine it?

"Abasi Mu-Udim" The Creator and Creations

That is where you have **THE FATHER GOD** meaning **THE FATHER IS GOOD**.

Blessed are the merciful for they shall obtain mercy. Blessed are the pure in heart for they shall see good – they shall see God. Good God – (*eti Abasi*) *but not* all *Abasi* is good. Not all Gods are good. God means Helper - something that can be helping. Your earthly father is your God. Your earthly mother is your God. Adam is called God the Father and Eve is also God the Mother. They are of the earth. Without your father you will not be a human being, you will not see the air and that means he is the creator on earth. That is what is called God the Father, The Creator is **The Father God** is **THE FATHER GOD** The SPIRIT itself.

I, THE FATHER GOD is this SPIRIT but **I** *refine* **MYSELF** to be **DIVINE** as the Holy Spirit. As the Holy Spirit of Truth, **I** have **MY** Truthful Self that cannot change from the origin.

I have done many creations
but all these things that **I** have created give **ME** *wahala* (headache).

I became plural by saying, "**Let US**" create this so **I** created this and **I** created that.

I created everything with **MY** curiosity

I created everything with **MY** busybody self.

I created many things with **MY** Love Self.

I created Heaven.

I created the universe, angels, this and that, so **I** become plural with Love. Love can make you do anything.

Now, all these things **I** created have grown wings and have become 'big'. Angel has become a big angel. Lucifer has become a big Lucifer. Everything has got big. In the spirit soul object of **THE FATHER**, they are big. And they then become problems. They all become a job to handle and became concerns but when **I** was **MYSELF** alone, did **I** have all these problems?

If you are a man and marry a woman, you have problems. If you are a woman and have a husband, you have problems. When you are alone that is, single as a bachelor or a spinster you can eat anything that like. You can go to anywhere that you fancy going. You can go out and come back at two o'clock in the early hours and there is no problem. You have no particular woman or man friend as the case maybe and no child. You live by yourself so you are free to go anywhere and do anything that you like. However, as soon as you decide to attach to a woman or a man, the questions come as:

Where have you been?
When will you be coming home?
When will you finish your job?
You know, you are not free, again–o!
Another question is – what will I eat?
Where is my food?

Even if the person does not ask, you will like to give food to someone you like and you will like to talk to the person. These are the problems of Love. Love problems!

Okay! When you are married, the order and instructions come as follows:

You can't do that job!

You can't go to that place!

You can't carry that woman everyday in front of the car! Oh you can't do this!

Oh you can't do that!

There is a lot of you can't you, you can't because you have attached a certificate to someone as an official wife or an official husband.

Okay, now you have children! Every child believes it is the responsibility of their papa and mama to take care of him or her, even if they are lazy and grown up. Oh, my papa does not talk to me. Oh my mama did not see me crawl. Oh, my papa and mama do not feed me.

"Abasi Mu-Udim" The Creator and Creations

These children were an object soul when you brought them. You do not know them and they do not know you, but it comes becomes your responsibility to look after them, give them food, tolerate them and do everything for them. You can't throw them away. You can't do anything to them. They hang on your neck and that is love problem.

Think about all these things and you will realise that as it is with **ME** with situations and things, so it is with the world as all activities reflect the same situations. There is no difference. People say, 'oh **GOD** has no problems! Who told you that **I** have no problems? Since **I** created you, do you know **ME**? Show **ME** one day that you man have worshipped **ME** in a respectable, correct and proper manner. As **I AM** talking now, is it not tackling a problem, so that you should know **ME**?

Since **I** created the whole world, how many people know **THE FATHER GOD**? How many people have even asked one day 'how did I manage to be created?' How did this thing or that creation managed to be? Show **ME** any president in the whole world that have sat down and reasoned and said, 'this world belongs to someone. Let me find a way to recognize that person being that I am of influence and I have all this power in my hand and

I command America

I command Britain

I command Europe

I command Africa

I command everywhere so let me use my influence and authority and command people to worship **THE FATHER GOD!**' Why can't they do this just as King David! Just as Abraham! Just as King Solomon who has commanded people to worship **THE FATHER GOD** again? That is **MY** problem as the **CREATOR!**

What **I** have created has bigger wings than before. They create nuclear weapons so that when **I** fly down, they drop it on **MY** head! They do all sorts of things – **MY** creations! What is Satan? What is Lucifer? It is **MY** problem. Who created it? Is he and she not part of **ME**? All that is **MY** problem, nonetheless, **I HAVE SOLVED THE PROBLEMS OF MYSELF** –

By loving

By being tolerant

By being patient and having mercy

By rejecting the back self,

By **MYSELF BEING THE FATHER GOD**.

I sat down and I said there are many raw materials and I have yet to produce something that will glorify **ME**. I had created Crude oil, raw gold, raw aluminium, raw diamond and others inside the ground but none of them created anything. It is you-man that has to refine them and use them for various purposes. For example, you refine crude oil into many things such as petrol, kerosene, gas and lots of other things. The same is applicable to many other raw materials that can be refined. And so it is with the world.

This **world** is **raw**.

The **SPIRIT** is **raw**.

And **THE FATHER** is **raw** but through a process, all can be refined so I refined **The Word**, the **Spoken Word**, the **Positive Word**, and **THE HOLY SPIRIT** through **MY** refined projected Self that I refined and became **GOD THE FATHER** in the physical world and **THE FATHER GOD** in the spirit.

And **GOD ALMIGHTY** – in-between **THE SPIRIT** and **THE FATHER** and the physical is **THE SPOKEN WORD, GOD ALMIGHTY**. That is why '*I AND MY FATHER ARE ONE*' as Jehovah God and His Christ, then man.

Everything **I** need is from man – Glory, Honour, Respect and all exaltations must come from man. '**ME** and man' will put 'leg in one leg of trouser together' since **I** created you for a purpose therefore every living soul on the surface of this earth from human-fish, human-bird and human-animal and those that become evolutional man to human-God, must sign up because this is the time. So, sign up today and if you don't then you have clearly signed yourself away from existence.

I have now declared **MYSELF** and made **MYSELF** known. **THE FATHER** and **THE FATHER GOD** is one thing. But **I AM** Improved Divine Consciousness as The Divine Self which is The Holy Spirit of Truth and that is **THE FATHER GOD**. And **I** want everybody to know through God Almighty who is the **SPOKEN WORD**.

I have earmarked The Universal Shrine who was Adam now, the King of Kings and the Lord of Lords called **GOD THE FATHER** on earth. HE is *Ete owo* –**The Father of** all humans in **GOD**, Olumba Olumba Obu.

C: THE WORD AND THE SUPREME WORD

What is **The WORD** and what is **THE SUPREME WORD**? You have asked yourself these questions because you want to know so **I AM** coming up with this information of **THE WORD** and **THE SUPREME WORD** just like **THE FATHER** and **THE FATHER GOD**.

It is **THE FATHER GOD** that will destroy the father of evil and all the people that practice evil and commit all sorts of atrocities by putting all evil in the lake of fire. Now say to yourself, *my* negative self that troubles *me,* that *my* arrogant *self,* this and that, which are not good, destroy them by your-self. If you don't fight and conquer your carnal self, your spiritual self can not win. Every evil lives in you until you conquer it. Just as Satan lives inside **GOD**, because **GOD** is the only one thing that exists and that is the old **FATHER.**

Now the new **THE FATHER GOD** with the new Heaven and New Earth has arrived and it is **RIGHTEOUSNESS, PEACE, LOVE, HARMONY, ONENESS, UNDERSTANDING, WISDOM, PERFECTION** that, have come.

No more wars

No more killing
No more fighting
No more hatred
No more lies.

And you must forget about all the things that you do that are evil because you will never succeed with them. If you bet **ME**, you bet **ME**, then bet yourself and bet **IWEUS**.

THE WORD and ***THE SUPREME WORD***: people say the Word is everything, because **THE FATHER GOD** says so. Yes! What type of word? There are words that people use to do incantations, fornication and other things. Everything is the word. That is the reason **I** command all words to celebrate **THE SUPREME WORD**.

The **Word** is a servant.
The **Word** is a slave.
The **Word** is Satan.
The **Word** is all and all.

All these words must come to worship **THE SUPREME WORD**. They must bow down and acknowledge **THE SUPREME WORD**. If you refuse this then **THE SUPREME WORD** will fight you and you will never conquer **THE SUPREME WORD, THE ALMIGHTY**

FATHER GOD THE CREATOR OF THE UNIVERSE.

Don't you know your source is the power? Destination has no power. Wherever the source of power comes from is where the power lies. If you make a mistake for instance, and your enemy fights you with juju and you also fight your enemy with juju but you do not ask yourself who gave your enemy his or her juju? It is the same person that gave you. So, if your enemy gave the juju man or juju doctor more money than you gave, then, the juju man will increase the power for him or her to fight you and win you over. What is the energy of the juju? It does not exist. It is his mind.

Therefore if it happens that you successfully bribed the juju man or he likes you more than the other man then his energy and his force of himself will stand by you more than your opponent and then you will win your enemy over the fight. That is the secret behind these things. There is no juju and no Satan of anything.

If somebody sits down somewhere and thinks well of you, it gives you more positive energy. The more people think well of you and support you, the more truthful you are and the more positive you are. All that energy of positivism and energy of thinking are your energy. And it is your energy and your force that stands with you. So, even if the whole world came to do evil to you, they will not succeed because you have thousands and millions of positive energies supporting you. And that is the power of **THE FATHER GOD'S** that is supporting you as the force of good will.

If you commit evil, especially hatred, each of the evil subtracts the positive energy of **GOD** in you then it becomes easy for evil to win you over. Show **ME** any powerful evil man on this earth that succeeds? There is none because another evil man will pull that person down.

THE WORD and **THE SUPREME WORD, THE DIVINE SUPREME WORD, THE CREATOR OF THE UNIVERSE**, the **ONE** you need to appreciate and honour is the **ONE** that gives you this message. This is not **The WORD** where you think differently and speak differently.

It is not the **WORD** that you have talisman in your pocket and you preach and shout Jesus! Jesus!

This is not the **WORD** that after you shout Jesus, Jesus you remove your pastor's cloth and go to the native doctor to give you power. And when you pay lots of money to the native doctor to give you the power, the native doctor will be laughing at you and by so doing,

You mock **GOD**!

You mock The **WORD**!

You are the accuser of The **WORD** and

The **WORD** will not respect you because you do not respect The **WORD**!

How many human beings in this world are truthful? The Word of Truth and The Spirit of Truth is **THE FATHER GOD**, the Holy Spirit of Truth. How many preachers are truthful? When you hear of this WORD, some of you will say you also preach, because you know all these things. Since you know all these things, what about the energy? What about the faith? What about the believing? Do you have any other thing attached to you apart from the **WORD**?

It is the **DIVINE POWER** that controls where this **WORD** comes from. But where do your words come from if you believe in any other thing? You are afraid of death.

Everybody is preaching. As a matter of fact, the job of preaching is the most lucrative work these days. Are you doing it for money or are you doing it to save souls? Are you doing it so that you can pay a heavy tax to the government for them to promote you? Shouldn't the government promote whatever is the truth, because government means **GOD**? Can't you see that a true government can never condone evil? The government of today however, condones anything and everything that destroys lives provided it gives them money to boost their economy so that they would say they rule the world well. That is the reason they support evil.

Which government of the world would sanction the production of cigarettes if they are for **GOD**? Which government of the world would sanction alcohol production if they were of **GOD**? Which government would sanction drug production (even though they pretend on the surface to ban them) if they are of **GOD**? They all sponsor the production of all these substances in a big way to get more tax and all that is evil but because no involved parties are truthful, they continue to perpetrate all this evil actions.

Even the church does not mind blessing a prostitute. Is that a profession? You see a beautiful girl come to you and pay heavy tithe in the church everyday but you do not ask her where her husband is? All what you do is say 'oh **GOD** bless you my daughter. **HE** will continue to make your work fruitful.' What work? Have you tried to find out where she works? Have you ascertained if she is married? You see a young adult well past the age between eighteen to twenty-five years and not married, yet appear to have a lot of money and you do not ask her what work she does? Rather you call that one a very good financial member of the church! It is the church of negative word.

'Oh what a huge and wonderful gesture' goes the accolade when someone donates money or builds a temple using blood money. Do you think Solomon used blood money to build a temple for **GOD**? **I** would not have accepted such a temple. When David wanted to build the temple with blood in his hands, did **I** take it? And that means you have to respect this **WORD** because where this **WORD** comes from is genuine.

Whether you are more knowledgeable than this or you preach more than this or are have more wisdom than this, are not of interest to **ME**. What **I** know is the *virgin* mind, the spirit, and the concept of where this studio generated this **WORD** because that is what **I AM** after. So, the **Word** and **The SUPREME WORD** are not the same but they are the same **WORD**.

Your words are raw words that are not refined. You curse with the same mouth that you use for blessing. You the same person goes to worship **GOD** and you the same person go to worship juju.

When Solomon worshipped **ME** and built **MY** *statute,* and eventually he went and did a pretentious dance with that woman, didn't you see **MY** action? Solomon did not worship that evil. **I** want to correct the people who wrote that because they did not write it well.

If **I** knew from **MYSELF** that Solomon really worshipped that demon, **I** would have killed Solomon in that place. The act was sightseeing. He pretended because he loved that woman and not the god of that woman. As he loved that woman he did that to please the woman and that was lack of understanding.

Today, you attach yourself to negativism blatantly. You use your money to promote negativism, and you think you are worshipping **GOD**. Do **I** accept rubbish? **I** do not eat from a plate that is not purely washed, no matter how palatable the food is.

Therefore, as regards **THE WORD** and **THE SUPREME WORD, THE SUPREME WORD** is the **WORD** of the Holy Spirit, The

Word of Truth, and the Word that lasts forever, just as what you are hearing now.

What will make this **FATHER'S TALK (GOD PRESENT)**; this information, last for eternity is because it stands for the truth, as the Word of Truth and therefore it is an Unchangeable Word. Even if you hate it now, tomorrow you will come back and love it.

It is The **WORD** that does not tell you to fornicate

It is The **WORD** that does not tell you to tell lies.

It is The **WORD** that tells you **to love one another**

It is the information that tells you to have peace, to have love, to have humility, equality, and treat everybody nicely and do not go to war, do not kill, do not segregate, do not practice tribalism and do not envy. This is the Word of peace, the food of peace for every soul. That is the information you are hearing now and that is why it will last as **The WORD** last therefore,

THE SUPREME WORD OF THE UNIVERSE should be recognized, appreciated and celebrated through out eternity.

D: THE CREATOR AND THE CREATIONS

The *Creator* and The *Creations.* What is the **Creator?** And what are the **Creations?**
THE FATHER is raw.
The **WORD** is raw and
The **Creations** are raw.

Just as **THE FATHER GOD**, the **Supreme WORD** and the **Creations** is the same thing.

The creation of GOD is this WORD. Through this WORD, I refine everything into different groups. For instance, personally, individually and singularly so that you can singular the truth out of evil.

Now everything is in creation -
Creation of **Love**
Creation of **Peace**
Creation of **Humility**
Creation of **Happiness**
Creation of **Mercy**

All these things are positive single creations that you can use to detect the fruits of the Holy Spirit. Equally all the creations that are positive are defined under that capacity there when you say 'it is **THE FATHER GOD** that created everything, therefore I can eat everything because everything is good,' you are wrong!

"Abasi Mu-Udim" The Creator and Creations

THE CREATOR knows that some creations are raw materials and some other creations are materials for the production of something. The farmer for instance, has seeds for replanting and seeds for consumption. The seeds for consumption and the seeds for replanting are kept separate.

The ones for replanting could be the over-ripe crop, which are good for germination. The production for consumption however, should not be over-ripped because when any fruit crop is over-ripped the potency of that fruit has gone back to the soil.

It is not good for anyone to interfere with life because every living soul's life is for replanting. Life is for continuation. Every life is for continuation. So, if you kill man you have consumed man then you have become the enemy of **THE FATHER GOD.** You have become the enemy of **THE CREATOR.**

All the four living creatures should not tamper with life. That is the reason **I** said, 'Thou shall not kill.' The instruction is not just for man not to kill man. If you can, do not kill even flies. Do not kill ants. Do not kill anything that is alive, because the word '***Thou shall not kill***' applies to anything that has life. Throw them away if you don't like them. Make a place and keep them so that you do not need to live with them.

Do not live with animals, because most of the insects are vampires representing animals, the evil ones and the blood suckers that are working as agents of Cain or serpent. Most animals are wicked. Even a rat is wicked. If you allow even a rat to live with you it eats your valuable papers and many other things in your house. If you allow cockroach or any bugs including other lower creatures to live with you they destroy things. Those are the things Satan uses to destroy things and fight the positive humans.

If you allow a snake to live in your house, it manipulates things in your house. If you allow mosquito to bite you, it eats your blood. It is a vampire. All these things are what the spirits angel soul employs to use to punish man. They are evil and negative.

If you live with a human being, especially a man of **GOD** in the house, he or she plays with you, makes you laugh, and makes you happy because he or she can go on errands and send messages for you. He or she will never be a stumbling block to you because that is the image of yourself and **GOD** and the likeness of **GOD** in your home and that is why human beings with life should be respected in all capacities. That is the meaning of *Creator* and the *Creation.* Man is the mini creator, while **THE FATHER GOD** is the **UNIVERSAL SUPREME CREATOR – THE SUPREME WORD, THE CREATOR OF THE UNIVERSE**.

Therefore, today you should know that you have the right of what you have created and **I** have the right for what **I** have created and what you created. What did man create and continues to create? Man creates everything that has nothing to do with life. That is, man creates artificial things and we will come to that in the Mundane (artificial) Part of this Lecture Revelation. That is what man created and creates and they are those that cause confusion.

I, THE FATHER GOD creates living things and spiritual things. They are part of **MY SPIRITUAL SELF** in creations, and because of that **I** have the power to control them so do not interfere. The worst enemy of **THE FATHER GOD** is when you interfere in the creations **OF THE FATHER GOD,** which is any living thing. Some instances of your interference are, changing **MY** creations. You try to modify humans, alter people, reform, reshape, modernise or do whatever with them or to them. You are the most insulting of persons. You are Satan in disguise. You can create aeroplanes and everything to make living possible and easy, but do not interfere with life.

Do you see what scientists and doctors do? As they want to take the job of **THE FATHER GOD**, they call themselves doctors and try to cut and paste. They take the gene of an animal and put it in fruits. They also take the blood of animals and give to women to give birth from. They have done so many things like that. If **I** reveal to you what human beings stay in the laboratory and at other secret places to do and plan to fight against **ME**, you will wonder. **I** allow them to do what thy do to see how far they can go in this world. And at the end of day **I** render them useless and empty. When they die that ends their activities and they will return back to their animal nature. They will not achieve their aim.

No human being will ever be able to succeed in creating another human being or another life. When you cut and paste life, you are a cursed human being. Leave life to be natural because Nature knows how to bring things out.

You can cure the wound of life. You can heal the wound of life. Man is a Helper because

"Abasi Mu-Udim" The Creator and Creations

man is God therefore when **I** create any living soul; take care of that soul as a caretaker and as a servant of GOD, because that is a part of you. Do not try create life because that is an insult.

If a woman gives birth, the mother and the father should take care of that child. They can massage through, love, affection and positive teachings but **I, THE SUPREME NATURE, THE UNIVERSAL SUPREME WORD** will lead man to grow according to what **I** want. You have a duty to care through love as soon as a human being is born, but you do not have anything to do with the life of that person. Nonetheless, there are some things you are to do.

I have so many medicines, which **I** created inside leaves and inside plants in so many ways to cure things naturally. It is not the ones you call drugs, which you purport to, cure people. Drugs are interruptions. They are fornication and virus, because when you make drugs, it is easy to inject powder or anything negative into it and give to somebody. Such are not the cased with raw medicines. An example of a raw medicine is that when you have a cold, you drink the tea of a ginger root and it would it will warm the inside of your body. You do not need to put anything inside it. Just crush, grate or cut them in bits and boil and drink. Should that lead to you making drugs?

I THE FATHER GOD has created so many natural things and if **I** give you the knowledge to know them then you should use them naturally. Some leaves in the bush are to drive away serpents and evil but instead of leaving them as they are, you cut them down to make drugs and other substances and when people take them, they become mad.

For instance, the leave that cocaine is derived from is to drive away evil. If the leaves stand somewhere or planted somewhere, evils spirits or ghosts or witchcrafts that are manipulation of invocation of ghosts, cannot go near there. The reason is that the leaves alone are hot.

But look at what Satan did. Since they do not want it to act in that natural way, they use these leaves to make drug for human consumption and when they take it, they become the evil. That is what is happening with so many other things like that which **I** can decode. But now the Holy Spirit supersedes all that. That is, why it is **I THE CREATOR** that knows the secret of **MY CREATION** in the whole universe.

E: WHO ELSE EXIST APART FROM THE FATHER GOD

Tell **ME** who else exist in this world and is in the scene of everything apart from **ME, THE FATHER GOD**. In the spirit, it is **THE FATHER GOD**. In the soul, it is **THE FATHER GOD**. And in the physical, it is **THE FATHER GOD**.

I make **MYSELF SPIRIT**.
I make **MYSELF WORD** and
I make **MYSELF** man.

That is why **I** gave the Lecture Revelation titled, ***THE FATHER GOD, GOD ALMIGHTY AND GOD THE FATHER*** and that means that,

In spirit, **HE** is **THE FATHER GOD**.
In the soul **HE** is **THE FATHER GOD**.
In the physical, **HE** is **THE FATHER GOD**.

This is the Trinity – spirit, soul and physical. And all this is **FATHER, FATHER, FATHER**! So, who else exists in all capacities apart from **ME, THE FATHER GOD ALMIGHTY, THE CREATOR OF THE UNIVERSE, THE SUPREME WORD**?

F: THE SPIRIT IS EVERYTHING

THE SPIRIT is everything because no other thing exists apart from the **SPIRIT.** And since everything emanates from the Spirit, the **SPIRIT** is everything. The SPIRIT is Brotherhood. You should not hate anything or anybody but you should not accept what you do not know either. Leave everything to everything. Let things be because it is only **THE FATHER GOD** that knows everything.

I THE FATHER GOD has not created any bad things on this earth. Bad things came out from curiosity of use and the way evil manipulates things. If someone hates you, that person can do wicked things to you. For example, you have prepared a pot of delicious soup but because someone hates you, they go and drop a quantity of kerosene in your pot of soup so that you cannot eat that soup again.

This means that evil has planted bad seeds among the good seeds so that when you come to notice that the seeds are bad, you will clear all the plants including the ones that are good. However, since **I** know the cunning of evil, **I** decided and said, '**I** will not destroy them.' **I** will leave both to grow and when they bear fruit, **I** will know which fruit is good and which one is bad and that is the reason, you see, **I** do not judge the world as **I** previously did.

Before now, **I** would destroy everybody and left one person and Satan would again go about through fornication and inject his virus amongst **MY** creations. Then everyone born thereafter would be worse than before, just as people, are worse now than previously because fornication is the virus that Satan uses. You know, Satan cannot actually come physically on earth because **I** put up to barrier to stop him by making him enmity with pregnant women.

There is no way Lucifer can be born into this world! She will never be born here on earth! She has so many evil spirit souls, and people that are her agents. She can use them, but she will never be born on earth, because that is the entrance into the physical world.

Since she will never be born on earth, what she does is to go about seducing the angels that are evil self. She uses them to spoil a lot of things and spoil a lot of people. She changes so many things and does all sorts of things and some are possible, because you accept the evil people around you. Nonetheless, the Holy Spirit surpasses all that now!

No other thing exists apart from **ME THE FATHER GOD** and since **I AM** everything and

I know everything therefore, this is the time that everybody is free.

The **SPIRIT** is everything, because without the **SPIRIT** nothing can exist and since you know that the **SPIRIT** is everything, bow down to the **SPIRIT**, accept the **SPIRIT** and accept what the **SPIRIT** says as final because it is the truth, through **THE UNIVERSAL SUPREME WORD.**

G: THE WORD '*LET*' AND THE WORD '*LET US*' THE GENERATION SPIRIT OF LIFE STAND FOR SPIRIT

The word **'LET'** and the words **'LET US'** are the force of creation and the force of the creation of Love and Cooperation.

I, THE FATHER GOD is love and **I AM** the **ONESELF** that coordinates all selves. **I** said, **'LET US'** and that **'US'** is the Generality Spirit of General. That is the one that is GOD as the Generality of The Existence of The Spirit, **The Singular**.

The spirit of love and all its components mean **GOD**. And that is what is called **Generation Spirit** as the spirit that makes things generate from time to time. That is the time that goes round and round and round and that is what is called **OOO**.

The Generation Spirit is **OOO**. It generates in spirit. It generates in the soul and it generates in the physical. Nothing that generates can have any other shape than **O** because it is round, like a ring.

Why should people argue about **OOO**? Satan does not like it because when the **O** generates it includes Satan and it controls her, and that means that she has no other place to go than to be inside **The Included**. The reason evil people do not want to hear about **OOO** and say all sorts of things against and about **OOO** is because the letter **OOO** is embedded with a Refined Divine Generation Energy. This energy is **THE SPIRIT OF THE FATHER GOD, THE SUPREME THOUGHT, THE SUPREME WORD IN THE SUPREME HUMAN GOD, THE FINAL SUPREME WORD PERSONIFIED, THE HOLY SPIRIT OF TRUTH.**

O – circle – ring is wonderful. It surpasses 666 and surpasses fox - xxx. *THE SUPREME LETTERS* OOO is **THE WORD** *LET US is-* **the Generation Spirit** and it stands for life and The SPIRIT. It is the **Generation Spirit** that gives life. The SPIRIT itself is the Multiplication Spiritual formula in nature.

Multiplication Spirit is the energy that gives the force of life to everything on earth, for continuity and for everlasting. **HE IS THE FATHER GOD. HE IS THE SPIRIT.**

When you reach this stage, then you have understood the actual thing that we are talking about in this Lecture Revelation and this means that everything has come to life.

The SPIRIT that reveals this wonderful secret thing is The LIFE **HIMSELF**. It is **THE SPIRIT AIR THE SUPREME WORD OF THE UNIVERSE** and The SPIRIT talks for **HIMSELF**. Without **HIM,** this will not be possible.

So, everything is the will of **THE FATHER GOD.** What **HE** wants is what **HE** has and what **HE** gets. And since it has pleased **ME** to *materialize* these words then **I, THE WORD has** exposed the SPIRIT which is, **THE FATHER, The Son, The Spoken Word** that is talking now as **GOD PRESENT and that means that** everything is well for mankind and GOD'S glory is actually materialized, in the name of our Lord Jesus Christ. Amen.

This is the end of Part One of **THE CREATOR AND CREATIONS – SPIRITUAL, NATURAL, MUNDANE OR ARTIFICIAL – THE SPIRIT FATHER GOD.**

THANK YOU FATHER. THANK YOU FATHER. THANK YOU FATHER.

In the name of our Lord Jesus Christ

In the Blood of Our Lord Jesus Christ

Now and forever more

Chapter Two

ABASI MU UDIM (THE BLESSED MOTHER
THE CREATOR AND CREATIONS

Part Two

"THE NATURE" MOTHER EARTH OR MOTHER GOD

FATHER'S TALK
(GOD PRESENT)

Christ Our Lord, Fifteenth Judas Iscariot, FATHER, Two Thousand and Eight (AE/OC/BOOH) Saturday, Fifteenth, March, Year Two Thousand and Eight (15/03/2008)

In the name of our Lord Jesus Christ

In the Blood of Our Lord Jesus Christ

Now and forever more

"THE NATURE" MOTHER EARTH OR MOTHER GOD

It pleases **ME, THE FATHER GOD THE CREATOR OF THE UNIVERSE** to bring out this Lecture Revelation, which is Part Two of **THE CREATOR AND CREATIONS: SPIRITUAL, NATURAL, MUNDANE OR ARTIFICIAL**

A: WHAT IS NATURE AND NATURAL

What is *Nature* and *Natural*? As previously in '**Spirit** and **Spiritual,** a similar question has come up again. What is **Nature** and **Natural?**

Nature is wonderful, however, some people do not understand this and as a result, they mix things up and down.

Nature is how everything physically manifests on earth. **Nature** is an object as how you can see objects physically. **Nature** is *OBU,* the physical hardware of the **WORD**.

The **WORD** formulated **Nature.**

And this **NATURE** is GOD ALMIGHTY which is **THE MOTHER GOD** as the one that people call **Mother Nature** which is the hardware of the '**WORD 'SPIRIT'** and it is very powerful. It is the foundation of this physical creation and that is why the physical world is based on **Nature.**

You can see **Nature** and at the same time it is **Spirit**. You can be looking at it, even keenly observing it whilst it is growing, but you cannot see the actual movement of growth. A human being is nature. It is a phenomenal nature that you can see a human being with your naked eyes and you can touch and hear the person but the person is growing, but it is also spirit soul.

This world that you behold is the **Nature World** as the **Natural Nature World**. And you can see that within the world, things are changing, but you cannot see the process of change with your observations. The **WORD** means **Spirit** and the **WORLD or UNIVERSE** means **Nature**. Anything **Nature** is Almighty. It is Supreme and that is, **THE FATHER GOD**, The Earth in the form of the **MOTHER EARTH**.

MOTHER is not different from **FATHER** in being raw and that is why **Nature** is very powerful and it brings out things to the physical as the force of creation because **Nature** brings things to the physical reality, '***THE HAPPENING***'.

Nature is the process of manifestation.

When ever **I, THE SPIRIT** wants to do something that is, when the **WORD** makes a pronouncement, the force of the process itself is the **Nature** and this is *NATURE* and *NATURAL*.

What is **Natural**? **Natural** means something that happens through the **Natural** way. **Nature** brings its own things and that is the reason that you should allow **GOD** to handle things, because they will work in the **Natural** way. The spiritual way is the way **GOD** does things that you do not know about, but when things want to come physically, it becomes **Natural** way. That is the **Nature** and the **Natural**.

Sometimes human beings do not understand this. If you are a man of **GOD**, allow things to happen naturally because natural is not evil. It is the original way of things, as the 'happenings' that no one can hold anyone responsible for therefore no one can be blamed because it is a **Natural** occurrence that happens **Naturally**.

I AM The Nature MYSELF and the force of **MY** will is **Natural** therefore you cannot blame anyone for that. No one blames anyone when **Nature** does something. When the **Mother Earth** does something, you hold **Mother Earth** responsible or you assign it to **THE FATHER GOD.**

THE FATHER means SPIRIT but **Nature** means **Mother Earth**. Every physical human being comes from **THE FATHER** in spirit, which is the air as **THE SUPREME WORD.** But when you come to materialize physically you will come from the **Mother Nature** which is **GOD**. And that is why you cannot live in this world unless you come from **THE FATHER GOD** and **THE MOTHER GOD,** which is **THE SUPREME NATURE**. That is the reason that you should allow for natural things, because they are the best.

You can see that natural food is the very best food, because **I** brought everything physically through Nature.

A human being that is born naturally is good, but the ones that are artificially born have problems. When you take medication to get a child or a child is planted inside you, it is affected by you and that is the reason that most people in the world are carnally inclined. They are artificial human beings. They are not natural human beings.

There are people who are born into the world naturally and that means that they are natural human beings who are spiritual. However, now, there are artificial human beings on earth and **I AM** going to explain what they are by expatiating on it.

Spiritual people are the people that **GOD** has sent. They are born through the inspiration of spirit soul, but they passed through Nature to come to this world. Adam was a natural man that **I** created in a natural way. That was the reason he was raw, but the spiritual Adam was Jesus the Christ, Our Lord. And the spiritual Adam that was Jesus Christ is The WORD Potency and that is the reason the WORD Potency can help the natural man. So, it is the spiritual humans that help the natural people.

Natural people have love. They are natural. They have sympathy. But artificial people cause problems. **Nature** itself can bring anything you put before the **Nature**. If a wicked man sleeps with a woman, she gives birth to a wicked child.

Serpent slept with Eve she bore Cain – natural. **Nature** is the force that forces things to happen by nature. It is what you put for Nature that **Nature** signs for you. It is only **THE FATHER GOD** alone that can detect what is what, but leave it for Nature. If you allow Nature to judge, Nature will judge in the normal way as the truth, but if you allow artificial and carnal minds to judge, you can make mistakes.

When people commit sin, Nature judges them, because a lot of people, who come to this world, came to support their spiritual nature. But when you come here and 'miss road' (miss your way), your spiritual nature deals with you. There are lots of things that happen naturally in this world that no one is involved with its happenings. A lot of people go mad naturally. A lot of people die naturally. If you allow things to happen naturally, there would be no problems in this world. The problem is that humans apply a lot of artificial forces to so many things and that is when you fight against **GOD**. And that is why mistakes are filled up everywhere in this world.

"Abasi Mu-Udim" The Creator and Creations

People say, 'oh without the force like the Police, Army and other forces things would be too bad in this world'. How can you believe that? How can you believe that without those bodies things would be bad in this world? **GOD** uses **Nature, the Supreme Nature** to control everything. **I AM** going to give a story now about what Nature can do to show you what **GOD** can do using the Supreme Nature to sort things out and put things in order.

There was a man in a place who was a King and had a son. Everybody loved this King but this King had only that one child, however the King was powerful and influential and people really loved him. People liked this king very much.

The King called a meeting and announced that he was going to send his son abroad to acquire some knowledge that will benefit the whole community and that. "What is the opinion of the palace committee?" The King asked. They had a meeting for seven days and finally came to a conclusion.

They came and said, "Our King, what we think that will really, really help the community since you love us, since you like us, since you think well of us is that

"Abasi Mu-Udim" The Creator and Creations

people die in this community a lot and we do not know what kills them and we want your son to go and acquire the knowledge to stop death. So, if there is any place he could go and learn about something that stops death, so that nobody would die again in this place that will be very good for us".

The King responded that, that was very serious and asked where such a place is. The King's son was also curious and asked, "Is there any place that such a thing could be learned?'

They responded that since you are the king everything is known by you and the King knows everything. The secret of the Kingdom belongs to the King; the King is ordained, therefore, the King should know the secret. Also that the king is supposed to know about such a place where one can go to learn about stopping death occurring, because so many people die in this kingdom and the king still remained alive considering that the King is a prominent and important person and also not young. He has seen some years. He was old, but the young and the very young died instead of him. In line with that reasoning, they believed that the king knows where such knowledge can be acquired so that other people would not die. The king said 'okay I will talk to **GOD**.*'*

Since **GOD** *had made him the king and* **GOD** *made him to live long* **HE** *will tell him where to send his son to go and learn how to stop death in this place. The King said they should give him seven days to respond just as he gave them seven days for deliberation.*

The King went and prayed to **GOD** *and* **GOD** *said to the King, "It is very simple. There is a place like that and it is only* **'ME THE SUPREME WORD'** *that can train your son and give him power to stop death in your community."*

King asked whether it is true. **GOD** *said 'yes it is true'.* **GOD** *asked the king 'do you believe* **ME'***. The King said, "Yes my Lord, my* **FATHER***, and my* **GOD***." Then the King asked* **GOD***, "How am I going to manage with the learning situation?"*

THE FATHER GOD *said to the King, "Send your son to go and stay with a* *prophet of **GOD** for seven years and serve him and during the seven years -*

He should not eat meat, fish or any flesh.

He should not tell lies.

He should not hate anybody.

He should love one another.

He should remain virgin and not to meet with any woman sexually.

*He should be honest and truthful to the prophet. After the seven years the prophet will bring him home to come and work for the community being that he would have completed his course. And **I** will give him the power from then to stop death in the community." The King asked is that all?* **FATHER GOD** *said yes.*

*When the king woke up from the dream, he called his son and told the son the dream. He asked the son, "Will you do this?" The son answered, Yes, Daddy. As you have given me the go ahead, I will go and stay with the prophet of **GOD** for seven years during which he will teach me everything."*

They prepared everything and at the end of the seven days the King made the announcement that in truth there is a *place like that. That place is to go to **GOD**. **GOD** who created heaven and earth has an agent office where **HE HIMSELF** goes there to train people. When people finish the training for seven years they would go to their community and nobody dies again. They live forever.*

However, the whole community must cooperate with that child when he comes back. Anything the child says is what they should obey and believe it. If they disobey then death would start again. "Will you all obey when the child comes back?" the King asked the community. They responded, "Yes, what we are after is that nobody should die." They made all the preparations and sent the child to this prophet.

On getting there the prophet said to the boy that the only condition here as, you know, is -

Thou shall not kill anything.

You must not eat fish and meat and any flesh.

You should be respectful.

You should remain a virgin and not to meet with any woman sexually.

*Love one another and worship the true **GOD** in your heart.*

*The child said he believed all that and that he came from the family of **GOD**. So he started to serve the prophet as a servant of **GOD** for the seven years.*

*This boy grew with knowledge and the respect of **GOD** and with understanding, love and wisdom. Then he went back home and everybody was happy.*

*As a matter of fact, from the year that boy started to stay with the prophet nobody died in his community but the community members did not think about this. Nobody thought of it or even mentioned it. Nevertheless, when the boy came back there was jubilation and joy. Everybody was happy and they made merry and dined well. They built a house for him to become the future king in that place as a Prince and a prophet of **GOD**.*

Three years passed nobody died in the community. One day Satan entered into one of the Palace members, and said, ah you people sit down here, and make merry and all that after all the money that was spent to send this boy to learn the knowledge what prove has he provided that he can do this job? If any of you should die, can he make you not to die? Satan entered into this one person to present this idea. They agreed and said it is indeed true. Look at that, we never even thought about such matter for the three years.

They did not even say that, oh for three years nobody has died. All they said was that for three years nothing happened for him to prove his knowledge. What if any of us died now, we do not even have any proof of what he claims to be and can do. So, what should we do now?'

They agreed that they should go and meet the King to discuss the matte because it was a security issue. We do not want anything to occur accidentally. Saying 'we must do democracy very well. We must plan this place very well. We need proper administration in this place. We have to put things in order. We do not want anything to come to us accidentally. There are so many enemies everywhere therefore; we want to secure this place. So, we must have a proof. This man must prove to us that he is capable of protecting us in this our community'.

The King said that it is true. That he too would like to know that but in truth the King never thought of anything like that, though.

*The king called his son and presented the matter to him. The son said, "No problem, as **THE FATHER** likes it." That became the slogan, which the boy brought from the training. **GOD** said to the boy, "If this did not happen, bigger things than that would have happened. Everything is the will of **GOD**."*

*So, when they asked the Prince any question, he would respond that, this question is the will of **GOD**. He reminded them that the condition attached to his going for the training was that nobody should think evil. Nobody should be of trouble to anybody and nobody should go to war with another person. And that is how this community has been living for so long and nobody died.*

During this time since they did not kill anything, they did not eat any meat, fish or any flesh and nobody died. Everywhere was quiet. Everywhere was nice but they said they are not sure of any situation, because anything can happen. They then came up with an idea. They said they had to bring poison so that someone would volunteer to take the poison and if the person that takes the poison died and he brought the person back to life, then they would be sure that the community was safe.

Then the question was asked, "Who is the person to take the poison?" They answered that the King should be the one, because he was the oldest in the place and he was the papa. That he should start from his papa. Some people objected to the choice of the King. The King said he accepted their choice because that in truth his son would not allow him to die. "He will save me." Some people said no, what if he fails and we loose our King? Let us not try with the King.

Then the other side asked the person they should then use. They responded that they should try the experiment with a cow because at least we used to kill cows and for celebration and since we no longer kill cows to celebrate, we should use a cow for that instead of human being. If the Prince brings it back to life then we will know that he can do same to human beings.

Somebody said 'no, a cow is too big for this. Why can't we use goat'? They said okay, let's use a goat then. They brought the poison and fed the goat and the goat jerked, jerked, jerked and died. They called the Prince and said, ah a goat has died and you know that we no longer eat meat. You know since you travelled nothing died. Why is that only three years since you came back goats start dying? You should bring this goat back to life. They did not tell him that they deliberately killed the goat.

The Prince said 'no, that it was the will of **GOD**. If the goat did not die a bigger something would have happened, something real big and it would have been a big lost to this community'. He was not aware that they first chose his papa to take the poison. So he left.

They were so annoyed. Then the initiator of the whole thing, the agent of Satan said. 'I told you, how can someone spend a whole seven years to train on how to make life that is – to make someone to be alive and you ask him to bring a goat *back to life, he refuses'. 'Would you do that type of thing when your first job after learning such a skill is only for you to make goat to come back to life'? He asked one of his friends. He added 'if I were the one I wouldn't do it. I suggested we use his papa or even I would have taken the poison'. Someone on the opposite side countered that, that's a lie. "I am not the one to kill you. Suppose this boy is not able to bring you back to life, what then? You will be dead."*

Their previous suggestion to use a cow was now accepted. "Okay let's use a cow." The agreed, they brought a cow and poisoned the cow. The cow too jerked, jerked, jerked and died. They sent for the Prince and said this thing has happened again. This time around it is a cow, not a goat and as you know cows are too expensive. Do your best to bring this cow back to life.

The Prince said, "No, it is the will of **GOD**. *Suppose this cow did not die a human being would have died. Something bigger than the cow would have happened, therefore, we should thank God, Since we no longer eat meat and so cannot eat the* cow, I suggest you bury it." The man left them.

They were so annoyed, particularly one of them, agent of Satan. He said, 'when I made my suggestions you people did not take my words seriously. Was there any mention of goat or a cow when he went for the training? Human beings were the things mentioned that would not die. Maybe his course did not include bringing goat and cow back to life. It was only for man, not animals. So, let us try with human beings. That was where trouble began again, because the argument was, who would be this human being?

The one that previously suggested that he could volunteer to die was told – hey, you volunteered you would even die to carry out this experiment, now this is it. He refuted it arguing that it was the Prince's papa he suggested and that yes the King should be given the poison.

They went to the King and said he had to take the poison. The King said, "No, I don't trust this matter–o! Since the goat and the cow they poisoned died and were not brought back to life, I am not taking the poison. If any other person wants to *volunteer and take the poison, the person can do so.*

*They left the King's Palace with annoyance and said they were going to hold another meeting. They fumed and pointed out all the time they wasted. It is true that this Prince cannot stop death. He just says, "It is **GOD'S** will. If this did not happen, a greater something would have happened." Look at the seven years training and all the contributions we made to see him through the course. And when he came back we were jubilant, danced and bowed down to him that our God had come back. Now look at it, he can't even make common goat – an animal to come back to life. How can he then bring man back to life? They taunted him and derided him and gave him mouthful of insults. These were directed to him from every city in his father's kingdom.*

*Then they made arrangement with 'area boys' gangsters and thugs). They asked them to kill the Prince and let it be **'GOD'S** will' that he died; since everything to him is **'GOD'S** will and as **GOD** likes it.' So, they planned for him big time!*

"Abasi Mu-Udim" The Creator and Creations

The Prince attends church regularly. So, every Sunday he drove his family to church and back. The road he drove his family through had a hill that led to a bridge. So, ten men on each side of the bridge lay in ambush for the man. They planned that on approach to the bridge after the hill; they would jump the man, drag him out of the car and kill him including all his family in the car with him. Then, we will see how he will come back and tell us it is 'GOD'S will.'

Enye! Odudu! Abasi mi! OOO! Zim! Zim! Zim! Assassu! Wonderful God! Positive! Positive! Positive!

So, they finalized their plan, ten able-bodied men on each side of the road with all their ammunitions for the execution. They hid by the bridge. On that particular Sunday, the man drove towards the hill but he had to go down hill on this side of the journey. Approaching the Bridge, the break cut off from the vehicle – **naturally***! I mean* **Naturally,** *the break of the vehicle failed. The car with speed gruuuh-gruuh-gruuuh swerved into the bush where they lay waiting and crashed kpoaarrh into* *them! They ran and then rushed back to him and exclaimed, "Oh, our Prince, what happened?" He answered that it was **GOD'S** will. He saw all of them and suspected something was afoot. Then he said, "It is **GOD'S** will. Suppose this did not happen something more dangerous would have happened to my family and me. Even the wounds sustained and the complete wreck of the car is nothing compared to something more devastating that would have happened to us." He started dancing with his family and the people that were to kill them joined with the dance and agreed that truly indeed, it is **GOD'S** will because if this did not happen, we would have killed you today-o!*

*Today, we have known that indeed, you are truly with this **GOD**. In all seriousness we were really determined and planned to kill you and throw you inside this river and to let it be your **GOD'S** will. We have now seen it is **GOD'S** will that prevails. Everybody bowed down to the Prince. They acknowledged to him that his father the King would have died but GOD'S will took it away. It is our stubbornness that made us lost the goat and the cow. So,* now we have seen that **naturally FATHER GOD** proves **HIMSELF**. *We will always worship and respect* **THE FATHER GOD,** *in the name of our Lord Jesus Christ, Amien!*

SO, NATURALLY, THE FATHER GOD IS THE ONE THAT DOES EVERYTHING NATURALLY! Anything that you allow to happen **naturally,** without you meddling with it then, **GOD** knows how to manipulate it.

Sometimes you have a headache so that you will not have a fever. Sometimes a little something happens to you so that a bigger incident will not happen. Anything can be anything. **Nature** is the administrator through the **WORD** and through the mind. The **WORD** is working with **THE MOTHER NATURE** and **THE FATHER SPIRIT**. When people for instance are somewhere thinking any evil about you, **Nature** can cause 'go slow' that is, hold-up or traffic jam on your way to stop you from facing the danger ahead. Anything can happen **naturally.**

People plan evil and do a lot of things to others. Do you know why some people die mysteriously or just like that? So many people who plan to kill you die **naturally,** before they even finished the plan. **THE FATHER GOD** is at work in this world. So, if you allow **Nature** to take its course in everything you will not have problems in this world.

If you believe that **I, THE FATHER GOD,** is **THE SUPREME NATURE** that does everything, then you have no problems. Sometimes As **I** say sometimes, people do not know why this world is still standing with nothing happening to the world. The reason is that **I AM** working **naturally**.

When **I** did not yet come in the form of our Lord Jesus Christ to die for mankind, **I** destroyed man without hesitation. **I** destroyed man at Noah's time. **I** destroyed Sodom and Gomorrah. In fact, there was not too much sin like this Generation of Fornication and yet **I** destroyed this and **I** destroyed that because sin is a heavy load on **ME.**

This world is like an egg resting on **MY** palm. **I** control it. **I** weigh it. It is sins that make the world heavy and sometimes when it is too heavy **I** drop it. But now because of love and because **I** died for man **I** put it on **MY** knees and **I** can tell you, it is still heavy-o! So, if the heaviness gets too much and **I** dropped it on the ground, will you blame **ME?** Change and let the **Nature** take its course.

When the sins and abominations committed by different countries, different families and different people are too much, disaster enters into such place and wipes them away. Sometimes it would not kill the human beings, but shakes them so that they would start life afresh. By then all rounds of evil would have gone.

Sometimes they build a centre for fornication and call it a Tourist Centre. Sometimes they build and develop the place and the place close to water where the *mammy water* comes as beautiful woman to fornicate and pass the instinct of fornication virus and all the evil things to the world, **I** destroy the place. **I** use hurricane and **I** use flood to damage the whole place and that centre will no more there. From time to time **I** shift the world with earthquakes. When **I** see that the sin is too much **I** shift a little bit and they would say earthquake has entered the place.

Do you know that hurricane, cyclone, fire, flash flood and earthquake that is, everything that happens naturally is **THE FATHER NATURE** doing a lot of things?

When **Nature** knows that a place sins too much and they do not want to listen to **GOD**, it finishes them. With that action by **Nature**, no human being takes the blame. If you do anything by yourself wrongly you will pay for it, but anything that **Nature** does is by nature. Are you going to blame **Nature**? Therefore, leave everything for **THE FATHER NATURE** and **I** will sort it out.

There is no power that can withstand **Nature**. One second of the blow of wind can destroy anything that man creates in this world. A small ball of fire can enter a huge place and destroy it. A single thunder can destroy everything. **NATURE** is **GOD HIMSELF** therefore, you should be fearful of such **SUPREME NATURE**.

You should be fearful of **THE SPIRIT**

You should be fearful of **NATURE** and

You should be fearful of the **SUPREME WORD** because **the WORD** manipulates **NATURE** therefore, **I** implore you to know the meaning of **Nature**, which consist of **The NATURE** and **The SUPREME NATURE**. They are **The WORD** as **I** have explained.

B: THE MOTHER AND THE MOTHER GOD'S NATURE

What is **THE MOTHER** and what is **THE MOTHER GOD?**

THE MOTHER is the Earth we are walking on now and **THE MOTHER GOD** is the positive Mother that produces the energy of the **Mother Earth** that is taking care of all the children on earth and she is not evil.

THE MOTHER HERSELF is mixed with all sorts of things including carnality, but **THE MOTHER GOD** is the positive energy that generates through **The Mother Earth** through which we have the pop-up sand which are all the food viz., fruits, vegetables, rice, beans like soya from which seventy-two million varieties of products can be derived.

Man should not interrupt any food products. They should allow them to grow naturally, because they are the body of Christ. They are the true body of Christ. They are the true body of the **WORD** as what came from 'LET' there be this and that be. It is the **Spoken Word** that pop-up the sand of the hardware of **The WORD** as **The Mother** that brought out the fruits and other food.

"Abasi Mu-Udim" The Creator and Creations

Anything that comes out of the sand is called the '*FUEL OF HUMAN NATURE*'. When you read the Lecture Revelation called '*THE FUEL OF THE HUMAN NATURE*', you will see this. The **Mother Earth** feeds lives through '*the Fuel of Human Nature*' by providing human beings with food that gives blood and energy for the soul and the soul for the spirit. Therefore, since **THE MOTHER GOD** is positive, do not abuse it by putting juju, by putting incantations and other things as sacrifice on this earth. When you do that you abuse **THE MOTHER GOD** and you are in trouble.

The placenta in a woman's womb represents **THE MOTHER EARTH**. That is something that is natural as the nature of **THE MOTHER EARTH**.

When a woman gets pregnant, the quantity of air, which is the Spirit **WORD, FATHER**, the Bubble of Creation, goes in to rest into the woman, in the soul object form and that germinates through the woman's womb. It is a mystery. A woman does not have a seed; therefore that energy must come from man to a woman, from above to the earth.

Scientists posit that a woman has a seed but this is a lie because a woman has no seed, but he has sensation. Man is created with the energy called naturally with *infusion instinct of creation* and when a man rest in a woman and over shadows her she becomes pregnant but people wonder how it manages to happen.

When you read some of **THE FATHER'S TALK GOD PRESENT** Lecture Revelations you will see the authority that is, the arrangement of authority of how things happen. You will see that the energy passes through the spinal cord to the waste of a man to generate the energy of life, through the heart, when the man drops that energy into the woman's incubator and becomes the bubble of creation through the star, **THE WORD**, which is the Gen of the Spoken Word germinates in the lab of nature as the natural lab of **THE MOTHER OF EARTH,** in the woman.

A woman represents **THE MOTHER,** while a man represents **THE FATHER.** A woman is called the Mother as The Earth. A man is called the Father as The Heaven. The new heaven and a new earth are a new man and new woman from Christ respectively.

When a woman gives birth and the placenta comes out, the placenta is supposed to be transferred back to the earth. But now, scientists use them as medicine and that is abusing nature.

"Abasi Mu-Udim" The Creator and Creations

So many things that the some of the Soft Skin Lighter man does (Whiteman) in the Western World are actually destroying Nature, and **NATURE** has them in mind to trouble them from time and years to come and onwards some scientists negatives ideas and many Worldly and purely carnal people will be destroyed, because they destroy Nature too much. **I AM** giving this revelation as a sort of remedy.

Humankind should stop destroying and interfering with nature. You cannot fight water. You cannot fight the air and you cannot fight the *land.*

The NATURE, THE MOTHER EARTH called **ME, THE FATHER GOD** for a meeting and reported that some 'Soft skin or Lighter skin human' races that call themselves scientists and technologists are destroying her. When they come to the waters, instead of allowing the natural flow of the waters they block her path. When they go to where natural things are, they destroy them and grow artificial ones. So they are in trouble. They are going to face serious problems on earth for their actions. And that is why **I** reserved **Africa** to be a **Natural Home** for everybody.

In future so many countries overseas will be lost and become water but the continent of

Africa will still remain because they respect Nature. Anyway that is not the topic of today.

However, **THE MOTHER NATURE and THE FATHER SPIRIT** that is, **THE DIVINE MOTHER and THE DIVINE FATHER** in the manhood and womanhood produces the influence of the **HOLY SPIRIT OF GOD** the personified **WORD** to save mankind. Then, **The Carnal Mother Earth** is the carnal part of everything causing lots of confusion in the world with her carnal people.

Therefore, every human being should classify themselves as either you are positive natural person or you are positive spiritual person. Or you are negative spiritual person and a negative natural person, it means you are a spiritual person or you are carnal person. That is what it is.

C: THE NATURE AND THE SUPREME NATURE

What is **The Nature** and what is **The Supreme Nature? The Nature** is the force that brings things into reality. **The Nature** is the source and the force of things that change in a natural way.

The Nature is the cause of natural events, while **the Supreme Nature HIMSELF** is the force. Natural events happen by themselves. Nobody plans them therefore, they are natural occurrences. And it is the **SUPREME NATURE HIMSELF** that forces things to happen, which is **GOD HIMSELF.** That is what we call **GOD** therefore, when you allow things to work naturally, you are giving respect to **GOD**.

Judgement can happen naturally and a lot of things happen naturally without you meddling. For instance, in so many places in this world, they make laws that you cannot accuse someone that is trying to kill you in spirit- soul or in the dream land because you can't prove it but, nature can prove it. However, since you cannot prove that people plan evil against you in their heart and it reflects in your soul so you have bad dreams; or that they use invocation to invoke you and try to be wicked to you so you saw them therefore you say that someone is trying to be wicked to you, they pretend it is not happening and not there, but it is there. They know it is there and even the people that doing these things will ask you thus, 'can you prove it?'

Enye! Odudu! And since you cannot prove it leave it, leave it for nature. Nature will prove **HIMSELF**. From today as you hear this Lecture Revelation, it means that this Lecture is born physically and **I** the **Supreme Nature** will **naturally** prove **MYSELF** to the whole world. A lot of natural things will happen to those who are witches and wizards, those who are wicked, those who use elementary and frustrated souls in dreams, elementary forces, invocation and magic to be wicked to people and destroy people's stars. **I** will also make things to happen naturally in a big way to expose some spirit object souls that come out from the water and other planets as the aliens that destroy this world.

You will see a lot of natural things that will happen in this world either positively or negatively to reveal events of nature in this world, in the name of our lord Jesus Christ. Amen.

D: **THE EARTH, THE SUPREME FORCE OF NATURE**

The spirit-soul of this world as the earth itself has **SUPREME FORCES** that allows things to happen and makes things happen. All these **Supreme Forces of Nature** are working for **GOD** and they are **GOD'S Selves**. They can be angels. They can be spirit-souls. They can be anything, even souls. Some trees are spirit objects that is, angels. Some animals are angels and so many things are angels naturally. There are other **Forces of Nature** as, thunder, hurricane, cyclone, fire, water and all sorts of things that **I** use **as the forces of nature** to sort things out in this world from time to time.

Because human beings do not respect **GOD** they assign things to **Mother Nature and Forces of Nature** but who is the force of nature? It is **THE FATHER GOD** and **I** use these things to sort things out, naturally which man cannot effect.

E: WHAT ELSE CAN CREATE APART FROM THE WORD

What do you think is the Force of Nature? What do you think of all the things that happen? They are so you will respect **GOD** and believe in **GOD**, because it is the Spoken Word that **I** used in creating everything including humans. And it is the **WORD** alone that can create and put things in order in the whole world. Do not therefore, toy with The **WORD** and do not mess about with The **WORD,** because the **WORD** is All and All and **HE'S** to manifest the glory of **THE FATHER GOD** in a natural supreme way therefore you must respect and honour **THE WORD**.

There is no other power that exists apart from the Supreme Force of Nature, which is *'THE SUPREME WORD OF THE UNIVERSE'* that causes manifestations. And that is why **I** say that everybody must celebrate **THE WORD**. Mankind should celebrate **THE WORD**, all the worlds should celebrate and the entirety of humankind's celebration must centre on **THE WORD.** Those who go to heaven should celebrate **THE WORD**. Those who go to Hades should celebrate **THE SUPREME WORD OF CREATION.**

THE SUPREME **WORD** SEASON is, and must be the NUMBER ONE SEASON CELEBRATION in the entire Universe. Every human being is a celebrant, to celebrate the self that is, you via **THE WORD.**

F: **THE WORD IS THE A TO Z, THE FIRST OF ALL**

When you check the Library you will see the Lecture Revelation titled '*A to Z*' – The First of

All – *Akpan Abasi*. The first in everything is the **WORD.** The first of all man is Adam who is **GOD THE FATHER** as, *Akpan Abasi* who is *Abasi*. The first Son of **GOD** is **GOD HIMSELF**. The first of everything is everything itself, because through that first everything existed, but that thing is alone, because its own self is not complete.

When you start to say one, two, three, four, five then you start to have many selves and that is when the energy grows. That is when wisdom is plentiful but when only A existed without B, C - Z, it was not complete. So, **A to Z** is the Completion. That is '**THE SONG**', A to Z.

The Song is **THE FATHER**, it is **THE WORD** and it is the **HOLY SPIRIT OF TRUTH.**

G: THE WORD '*LET US*' AND THE MOTHER EARTH THE SUPERNATURAL SPIRIT OF INCARNATION BIRTH STAND FOR ENERGY BLOOD

I AM going to expatiate in this part a bit. The words '*LET US*' and **the Mother Earth, the Supernatural Spirit Soul** of incarnation, birth stands for blood. That is the reason nobody can make or produce blood no matter what.

Scientists and all of you whatever you are, you cannot manufacture blood, because blood itself is supernatural. It is supernatural because it is from spirit to spiritual and from spiritual to supernatural.

The mother earth, the force of nature of this world is supernatural. The energy that generates the air is **ME THE FATHER GOD** that produces life and gives existence to all humans and makes living creatures and organisms alive is supernatural. That is the energy that evil people, soothsayers and the like, tap and use in an elementary way and call themselves witches and wizards and all those negative names. That is the energy *animals* were using to cause the spirit- soul of witchcraft so that when somebody dies they use that to invoke the ghost.

The supernatural stands for incarnation world, the world of ghosts, and the world of souls for rebirth. This is the only area that can be manipulated. Some things come to this world as human beings, but they are not human beings and most of these problems are caused by angels.

When Christ did not die and the Holy Spirit had not taken charge in the world, **I** sent angels on errands to give protection and stand on the air, but human beings would bribe these angels to use them. They used them to give visions so they revealed so many things to humans. The angels told them what they could and couldn't do. They taught them magic. Humans seriously bribed the angels, made sacrifices to them and they left **GOD** for the carnality of the world. With this knowledge, but no understanding humans started to perform supernatural things, which were not positive.

The real **Mother Earth,** which is not different from **THE SUPREME MOTHER GOD,** is the Spirit-soul of this world that is supposed to help the people that manifest in this world to survive and help the world to grow in positivism. That is the force of nature that when it produces anything, it works in its proper natural way, but people use magic, incantations and all that for other things that are not positive. And this is the spirit object soul that people sacrifice to.

The sacrifices are not for **THE FATHER GOD** and not for **THE SUPREME MOTHER GOD.** They sacrifice to this supernatural object that is the soul that takes bribes. It is just like a situation in which it is not easy to bribe a President or King, but the subjects can be bribed. And it is only the subjects that can get around the King or any principal person to do some business. When your servants are not truthful they do a lot of business behind you.

Therefore, the spirit-soul of this world that is supposed to corporate with the Spoken Word to maintain everything that man sees that **GOD** created is now causing lots of confusion. That is what Satan has been using just as it used serpent to deceive Adam. So, it uses all these angels and ghosts to do all sorts of bad things and establish all sorts of evil things.

I AM A *SUPERNATURAL TEACHER*. And this Lecture Revelation you are hearing now is **SUPERNATURAL WISDOM** as the **SUPREME WISDOM OF GOD**. Anything that you see physically which is not ordinary is **supernatural** and **I** use it to help many people because it is spiritual and positive.

Supernatural is of two types. One is natural positive and the other is negative. The positive one is truth and the negative one is bad, which **GOD** will destroy.

Therefore **supernatural** can be both good and bad. So many **supernatural** occurrences have happened that have brought good things to human beings. If you do not come from a **supernatural** object, you cannot do anything in this world that will benefit another person. In this world if you are a mystic person, then you either a positive or a negative one.

His Royal Majesty King Solomon David **ETE** is a born mystic man. He is a mysterious man from the time of Abel till today and so many spiritual objects, souls and angels work under Him. Angel Michael reports direct to the senior spirit-soul after Lucifer. He reports to the record keeper, which is Abel and who is King Solomon. That was why when Solomon came to the earth he gave him a ring to supersede all evil. And now the Holy Spirit is on earth and has given Solomon the spiritual power to bring out information called **Comprehensive and Ability Memory of GOD** and this is in Him. He controls everything that is positive. And all negative things bow down to positive things because nobody can fight wisdom. Wisdom is the certified energy of **GOD** because **GOD** owns wisdom.

Wisdom is correct and Satan is mistake.

Wisdom means love but Satan means hatred.

Wisdom means peace; Satan means trouble and war, problems and arrogance.

The Wisdom of **GOD** is positive in all directions and in all aspects therefore no evil can conquer positivism in a fight.

Natural blood generates from the incarnation world to birth, the Hades, THE SPIRIT as, **THE FATHER GOD.** When **I, THE FATHER GOD** bring out the bubble of creation from the spirit of **WORD,** it is passed through the soul world to take an object formation and arrangement for the birth to take place is the incarnation world. And that is where you come from and where you return. Every object must come from there as imagination and go back there after the picture has taken place. When the object is no longer in physical, it is in imagination object soul as a shadow soul. The shadow soul of human life or anything that has life is what is called ghost.

Anything that has blood turns to be a ghost at their life expiration but when people are forced to die unnaturally, they cannot rest. When a life is extinguished by force, being that life has ghost, the ghost still hangs around to do certain things. That is what people use as magic. The reason people kill cows is to get accidental souls to work for them as energy. When you kill a man such as all the people that die in wars their souls haunt people and so does the souls of children that have been aborted as their souls haunts the mother of father that committed the abortion.

Many people suffer particularly women who get rid of the formation of a foetus in their womb after seventy-two hours because they have killed. You have committed murder and deprived a soul of existence therefore, that soul will fight you. Do not forget that this soul that wanted to come is already a human being that has a destiny and they are everywhere. When you deprive them of life, they war against you and that is the reason there is so much bad luck and problems all over the world.

I gave a revelation called '***The Spiritual Consequences of Abortion***'. Abortion creates bad-luck for any woman that in involved with it. So many men have bad luck and so many women have bad-luck and sicknesses because of abortion. What happens is that if a woman commits ten abortions, she has ten wounds in her system, because anything that is plucked out by force when it is not ready to fall leaves a mark of wound. You can experiment on this with any unripe fruit like orange or mango or pear and so on. Try to pluck out the fruit when it is not ripen. You would see that you will have to pull it hard and that leaves or even the twig could dislodge with the fruit. If the fruits however, are ripen any slightest touch and the fruit fall off. Sometimes you don't need to touch them. They just fall off the tree when they are ripened without taking any leaves or twig with them. And the tree will still be healthy. This is quite different when the fruits are forced out from the tree. The wounds on the tree will cause the tree to be unhealthy.

That is a similar situation to a woman. A woman that committed abortion has wounds not just from cutting off or forcefully plucking out the forming baby inside her but all the associated organs are affected and they all add to cause the woman lots of problems.

So, some women can be so beautiful in the body, but internally they are sick. And any man that goes into that woman gets one problem or the other. It could be bad-luck, internal heat and other things. A woman that committed abortion could have internal heat and sometimes it would not be possible for that woman to get pregnant again naturally. Some of them could be unaware that that was what blocked them from getting pregnant.

If the child you were pregnant with was powerful in spirit soul or a strong nature, could the person was your grandpapa or grand mother or any close relative and you barrier the person from coming, then you are in trouble.

That is the reason **I** gave King Solomon David **ETE**, ability and revelation to sort out abortion problems and make peace between the frustrated souls and the women that barrier them not to be born into this world. When you do that your star is corrected and you will have a child. This can only be possible if the woman spoke the truth. Some women could be stubborn and would not speak the truth. In that case there is nothing that can be done.

So, some men get bad-luck, because when you are sleeping with a woman that committed abortion, your luck is blocked. Not by the woman per se, but those frustrated souls come to you. It works like witchcraft. It works like evil, demons. They are not matured spirit soul so they behave anyhow.

The immature spirits souls are just like children that scattered things in the house and would think they were doing well. They will scatter things in your office, papers and all. They work like rats and all the destructive things because they never took mature evolution. They are still under primitive age of souls, when they terminate them. So, because of that they do lots of harmful things in the whole world including the governments, countries, companies and all. They cause so many problems. They can enter into somebody to go and kill naturally. This is possible, because they are spirits soul object and can take assumed body, when they are so frustrated, especially those souls that had only the last chance to come into the world. When a mother abuse that nature by committing abortion thereby stopping such soul from coming into the world they stay there for life to frustrate people, because they cannot come again.

It is just like when you have an important occasion and the film in your camera has only one slot left or the last cassette or something like that. Meanwhile, the occasion is still very much underway, but you can no longer take photos, because of problems with the camera or no film or no more memory left if you using digital and nothing available for download. Or sometimes you took some pictures, but they are not developed, you cannot use the same film to take pictures again, because the films inside are already exposed. That is a similar situation with aborted foetus. The film is exposed and can no longer be used to snap pictures.

As for those who call themselves medical doctors in the hospital and are involved with termination of pregnancies, you are just like a native doctor in the village that kills people in a diabolical manner by using juju or witchcraft. The same native doctors are born as medical doctors. They are only improved version of what they were in their previous life. They still do wicked things, but can also help those they want to help.

Therefore, if you are a native doctor or a medical doctor and you can do anything to help mankind, make sure you do not do negative things, do positive work. If you do negative work then you will pay for it.

Nobody is authorized to commit abortion. If a woman met a man and missed her menstruation for seventy-two hours, she has already entered into the cycle of development. If you take the foetus away by force then you have committed murder. If it happened naturally then you have no query to answer.

The channel of the womb of many women that committed abortion is affected, because of the force of plucking out the forming baby inside. In contrast, if a woman gave birth naturally, nature would close back the channel naturally and the woman's womb is not affected because nature does things correctly. It is life. It is a spiritual nature.

"Abasi Mu-Udim" The Creator and Creations

Some women even when giving birth in the hospital and they are given a cut their channel is affected. Or if they went for some other thing to do with the womb, could be abortion or some other thing to the womb, they no longer have natural channel. They are interrupted. This could result in miscarriage in subsequent pregnancies. They would take in the morning and in the evening the pregnancy is out.

Abortion causes miscarriages a lot, because nature is no longer correct. It is like a tree that has flowers and any slightest touch or shaking the flowers falls off. When the flowers fall off without yielding any fruits, that tree will never bear fruits again. That is what happens with some women. They are nice physically, but internally they are ill, with internal heat and serious headache with lots of pimples on their face and craw-craw everywhere on them. The cause is that when the blood does not flow properly it causes internal heat, which brings out lots of things from the body to the surface.

I gave the remedy to this to only one person, who was the first person that died through murder. He is the person that can appeal to **SUPREME NATURE** to pardon a woman who committed abortion. That person is His Royal Majesty King Solomon David **ETE** in all ages.

"Abasi Mu-Udim" The Creator and Creations

If you have committed abortion in anyway sort it out first.

Before you marry a woman ask her to be truthful if she had committed abortion before in her life. Also you are a woman, before a man marries you find out from him if he had shared, partook, contributed in anyway the committing of abortion before. If you are a man and you married someone who has committed abortion, it will cause lots of 'go-slow' that is, hold-ups in your life. Likewise a woman that marries a man who has committed abortion, there will be 'go slow' in your life. So many women cause bad-luck to men and so also men. They cause bad-luck to women.

If you employed a girl who has committed abortion and maybe it was a strong soul that she got rid of, that can close the office, because of bad-luck. Equally, so many offices close down because of fornication. Some of the offices that involves personal business when they committed fornication in the office, the office closed down, because the energy goes there and fight and close down the place, unless of course the office was established by evil.

If it is a government, it will bring problems and misunderstanding in the office, but the government office will not close because government surpass everything.

I AM giving this Lecture Revelation as part of remedy to help so many people with so many problems. Ordinary confession will not solve the problem of abortion because it has something to do with blood. It is only the blood of Jesus Christ through Abel and Stephen that can appeal for forgiveness on your behalf. Or your parents that is, your mama and papa who has nothing to do with blood. That is because **the Mother Earth,** the Supernatural is the spirit soul of incarnation birth. It stands for blood. That is why **I** revealed this lecture.

In the name of our Lord Jesus Christ

In the Blood of Our Lord Jesus Christ

Now and forever more

THANK YOU FATHER

Chapter Two

ABASI MU-UDIM
THE CREATOR AND CREATIONS

PART THREE
"MUNDANE" ARTIFICIAL OR MONEY

FATHER'S TALK
(GOD PRESENT)

Christ Our Lord, Fifteenth Judas Iscariot, FATHER, Two Thousand and Eight (AE/OC/BOOH) Saturday, Fifteenth, March, Year Two Thousand and Eight (15/03/2008)

In the name of our Lord Jesus Christ

In the Blood of Our Lord Jesus Christ

Now and forever more

PART THREE

"MUNDANE" ARTIFICIAL OR MONEY

Today, it pleases **ME, THE FATHER GOD THE CREATOR OF THE UNIVERSE** to give this Lecture Revelation, which is the third Part of **THE CREATOR AND CREATIONS: SPIRITUAL, NATURAL, MUNDANE OR ARTIFICIAL**

Today, **I** want to explain what money stands for. The **mundane** stands for money and that is artificial energy. Man created money, not **GOD**. Nonetheless, man is **GOD**.

It is only when man uses what he created in a positive way that man glorifies the **ONE** that created him. But when you use it in your own negative way you do not glorify **GOD**, then it becomes a problem between **ME, THE FATHER GOD THE CREATOR OF THE UNIVERSE** and you.

Mundane glory is for man. Man created money and that is what **I** call artificial glory. Artificial god is money that man created, which some worship, just as human beings worship idols. They created idols and attached energy to it.

Mundane gods include idols and money. The actual mundane god that is controlling the world now is money called Mammon (CARNAL) of DEATH. The money itself is not bad, but the energy and the manipulation, being artificial, something that has no life that is the cause of problem in the whole world.

Today, **I AM** revealing the god of this world called **Mundane** as mammon which is as **artificial** as **money.** The way **I** treasure life, as human beings is the same way that the Imagination and the Idea of this world treasures money. The way **I** use man's life is the same way the Idea of this world called **mundane** uses money. So, life must be in man and the money also must be in man, before man's life becomes reasonable on earth. But what is the problem?

A: **WHAT IS MUNDANE?**

The **Mundane** is the carnal way of doing things, the carnal instincts and carnal influence. It is not Satan. It is only that Satan uses mundane things to manifest its glory, but **Mundane** is not Satan. It is a carnal thing as an artificial creation. It is mundane, but you can use it to glorify **GOD** if you are a positive person.

I, THE FATHER GOD THE CREATOR OF THE UNIVERSE gave man carnal knowledge to do the mundane creations.

An Aeroplane is mundane because it is a carnal thing. A car is mundane and a house is mundane and money is the head that controls mundane energy.

So, will you tell **ME** it is the work of Satan? It is not the work of Satan. Satan only uses money just as **I, THE FATHER GOD** uses the Word, the life in you.

People say, oh **GOD** says **HE** does not want money. That is a lie! Today **I** want to declare **MYSELF.** It is not Satan that created money.

She is only trying to use it because she knows that the more money she uses to influence people and sponsors a lot of carnal things the more she is likely to get more vote, but she will not win. She will always be in opposition until that negative energy is finish.

Satan will never win and will never rule. She is the master and leader of the opposition party. When a party cannot produce a president that is, a winner in an election it is a pity. They would change their chairman or president every second, reasoning that maybe the problem is from the president. They do not know that the president is not the problem, but the manifesto of the party is the problem because the concept, the scenario, the formation as what the party stands for is not what the citizen wants.

This aspect of this Lecture Revelation will put every politician and every party in this world right. What the **mundane** government calls politicians is what **I AM** going to reveal now as what they stand for and is what **I AM** going to reveal now and also what the money stands for is the **Mundane Kingdom**.

GOD represents **HIS** ruler ship with Kings and Queens or anyone that has spirit of GOD through the Divine Wisdom, but the Kingdom of the world represents with the **Mundane,**

Artificial which is **Money**. The most forceful situation is money as Hijacker energy. Anybody that has lots of money and worships money can do anything evil. Satan can use the person and **GOD** can also use the person to manifest **HIS** glory.

Before **GOD** uses the money to manifest his glory, the person **I** would use must have higherself, an awareness of himself or herself and have higher consciousness and know about **THE FATHER GOD** because without that the person cannot do it and that is the reason **I** said, "Seek ye first the kingdom of **GOD** and other things shall be added unto you."

What is the Kingdom of **GOD** you must seek? The truth life of the Holy Spirit, how to think well, speak well, hear well, see well and do well, you must pass through generation upon generations and acquire the power to love one another. Go through all narrow ways of life; pass through the tests of Natural Brotherhood, Physical Brotherhood, and then spiritual Brotherhood in many ways. When you conquer and have Love, Oneness, Mercy, Kindness, Righteousness and Faith in **THE FATHER GOD** and be Peace Maker, have understanding and know yourself, then that is the beginning of Wisdom, then **I** can put you in the position to be affluent and be in the mundane world. Then from there you would use that spiritual backup of yourself with spiritual consciousness to rule everybody with peace and love and with equality and represent **THE FATHER GOD**. Apart from that you are representing Satan.

Satan does not exist, but the mundane kingdom works for Satan and if you refuse to work for Satan then that mundane kingdom, becomes **GOD'S** business.

So, **what is** *Mundane*?

Mundane is carnality, as something that you copyright which is counterfeit, as something that can be useful but it is not real, a temporary approval.

Mundane is something that is not from the spiritual source. It is an imagination that has no base in the spiritual aspect of things, but it can be here. Money has no base in spirit-soul so if you base money in the spirit-soul you cannot have it, unless you use evil ways.

Money has base here on earth. Money is bestowed on the select few that is, in the hands of a few people that GOD bless with, but these people that use it are controlled.

In contrast, **GOD** is love. **HE** does not control people that use all the things that **He** created. For instance, everybody breathes the same air, enjoys the same sunlight or daylight. At the break of the day everybody uses it equally. A woman gets pregnant and gives birth here as well as another woman elsewhere. A rich man may not have any child while a poor man has eight to ten children. That is **GOD'S** nature. Nature does not say oh you are rich man so have children. If the mundane world controlled birth, they would say to you that if you are lucky to give birth to one only child then that is ok because you have no money but they will give one million children to the ones that have money because people have lots of money and they don't know what to do with it. This shows you that the mundane world is different from **GOD'S** business.

    The mundane is an artificial system as something you must force yourself to make, with their motives and cunning intentions.

    And the **Mundane** is what actually fights everyday against the spirit and natural things. The enemy of the spirit is the natural that does not understand things properly. Then, the enemy of natural is mundane that, does not allow things to work in a natural way. That is exactly what it is in this world.

B: **THE EARTH AND MUNDANE GLORY**

The earth and mundane glory are the things that are causing problems between Gods and humans. Since **I** created man in the image and likeness of **MYSELF,** man is supposed to listen to his own 'self' and listen to **THE SPIRIT** and listen to the voice of **GOD** in himself and do exactly what he hears in a positive manner.

But today, because of the situation of the mundane world human beings do not even listen to their self anymore. Using carnal love as a case in point, so many families want their children to marry rich people and not the people that they love. When a child says to their parents that; 'oh, mummy, daddy I want to marry the girl or the boy I love'. The parents will shush the child and ask 'what do you know about love? We don't have money and we don't have a house. We are suffering, because we do not have money and you are talking about love when the object of your affection is not rich'.

These parents have finished their lives and they don't care about yours own. When you check their history, you will find that when the two of them met, before they gave birth to you love, was first in their agenda. Now that it has come to your turn, they want money. That is an example of how the mundane world has improved from its previous situation. People say, oh what a civilised world! Oh modern world! **Modern World** actually means **Mundane World.**

What actually is the meaning of Modern World? What is the meaning of civilization? Civilized in what? In love or in humility? People are fighting now more than how they used to fight.

In the early time, they used bows and arrows for fighting and going to wars so it took them a long time to plan and the King had to lead the fight. But now Presidents and kings sit down at a place and make nuclear weapons that would go to shoot miles away. Then they would render their target country impoverished and they incessantly drop bombs on them while these people don't have food to eat much more buy even one bomb to shoot back.

So, this is the cunning of this world. Unless **I, THE FATHER GOD** intervene to sort this world out, things will get worse still. If this world continues like this for another one hundred years people will hate it when they are born into this world.

Even, now if **I** allowed what the evil people plan to implement to happen you would hate yourself in this world. The world would have been so bad that you would see lots and lots of people committing suicide, because if you are peaceful person, you would not like to live in this world. If you are an honest person you would not have survived in this world.

But everyday they talk about fraud, terrorist, killings and all other ills of the world. Who caused all these things? Who trained people for these things? Who made all these things to happen? They caused problems indirectly and come to offer solutions to make you feel bad that, you are the one that is bad. These are the world's problems. The energy of money in the mundane system is causing all this. It is not human beings. It is the artificial ideas that they have created. It is like dressing up someone as a masquerade and giving the person knife. When the inspiration of ghost or something enters the person because now you have influenced the person he would charge at you and at people and behave erratically using that knife that you have given him.

Let **ME** tell you a story of something that happened in the mundane creation. Artificial creations yield the energy of destruction. That is what people use to establish the secret societies and all sorts of evil things. They use the imagination in their mind to cause something to be or to create something. Being that what they create is evil and evil has no resting place it would go nowhere. So you can't send it away if you need to get rid of it. That evil would start to hammer and trouble those that caused it to be and kill them and destroy them if no more sacrifices are offered to it. It becomes evil around them, because they need energy to make that thing to survive.

This family scenario analogy should give another insight of dabbling into evil activities.

You don't have a child, but when you have a child you have created an abstract external energy that you need to see it survived. You have to understand ways to make the child sleep. You have to know how and when to feed the child. You have to know how to care for that child generally. They are all additional things to do, because of what you have created.

It is true that nature gave you the child, but you are the cause of creating it. If you did not sleep with a woman and get her pregnant, you would not have the child, therefore, all that is part of you.

Another instance is when you go and borrow some money to do something and you agreed with the repayment of double the amount borrowed. They lent you the money, one to enslave you and another for control. At a point it became too much for you and you could no longer meet with the repayment. It becomes a problem. Pay back the money – problem. Do not pay back or cannot pay back – problem. That is the mundane world for you. That is the kind of things that happens to make life difficult for people.

The mundane glory, the mundane systems cause lots of problems in the whole wide world. And unless **I, THE FATHER GOD** takes control you cannot succeed in this world.

Man manipulates the mundane world causing problems, but **GOD** can solve the problems if man knows **GOD** and surrenders to **GOD**. If you surrender to **GOD**, **GOD** will use his love and make things work well for you. However, if you do not listen to the spirit of **THE FATHER GOD** and allow evil to overtake you, you will create evil for yourself and the mundane energy as the artificial energy will disturb you and you cannot escape if **GOD** does not come to your recue. You will be involved in bloodshed and other evils and you will not be able to escape if do not listen to **GOD**.

The short story is that:

"Abasi Mu-Udim" The Creator and Creations

There was a family and the father of this family was a hunter and a fisherman. He used to catch big fishes and killed animals. When they ate the animals and the fish they kept the bones at near by place in the compounds so all the heaped, skulls and the bones of the animals and fishes they ate was in that place and they called the place the bone area. Why couldn't they scatter the bones or simply threw them away instead of heaping them up at a place and giving the place a name.

One day, the first son of that man had a dream. He had a dream that these bones were talking. One of them stopped and called itself 'utah' which means chew *and it said that it wanted a hot drink poured for libation. It talked, but this boy was confused because it did not see any human beings, but those bones that were talking. And one of them said again – 'my name is 'utah' meaning* chew *which means they have eaten the flesh and left the bones. So, then the bone called itself 'utah.' Do you know the meaning of that utah? It would have killed people and ate human beings if he had poured hot drink like Scotch whisky, snaps or some other similar 'hot' drinks on the ground for libation for that utah. That energy would start to grow and kill and eat people.*

*He had this dream the first time. When he woke up he said no, it can't be and he went and scattered the bones. He did not tell anyone the dream, but he went to see one native doctor. When he went they were doing their native prayers and as he approached the scene energy of that utah 'caught' the native doctor and said that it is, the soul of those bones that has entered into the native doctor and he started talking saying as he is that bone, 'I am the '****utah****'. He mentioned the same thing the boy dreamt about. 'I want a drink poured for me'. When the boy reached home, he collected the bones and threw them away and said nonsense! 'So I will start to worship bones now. After asking for drink the next thing it would ask for chicken, after a chicken it would ask for a cow and after that it would want a human being. And if you do not give it, the energy would start to kill people.*

And this is exactly the same way people do in secret societies and other negative practices. People create things that are not positive through anything you speak in the word. Even if you carried a piece of paper and start to pay attention to it, you have created energy therein. However the problem with these energies is that because **I, THE FATHER GOD** did not create them, **I** do not and will not give them any maintenance because they did not come from **ME.** They are external things that you need to feed and it this feeding that results in sacrifices and all the things that people are doing.

When King Solomon was King James in the United Kingdom, he worshipped **GOD** of Israel, the original **GOD** - The True **GOD**. Then they planned and brought the dragon child from China, the Egyptian mummy from Egypt and Indian gods as negative powers to come into the kingdom. This is a secret that **I AM** revealing. It is in **MY** records and **I** remember it because King Solomon **ETE** was King James and **I AM** the one that knows Him.

As **I** was saying, there were arguments when they brought those things and King James said he could not and would not worship those gods, but the real **GOD,** but they worshiped these things and that was the first thing that happened in the United Kingdom that led to **MY Holy Spirit** leaving the place from that time.

"Abasi Mu-Udim" The Creator and Creations

They seized these things as seizing power wherever they went. Whenever they want to seize control people, they would first capture seize the people's power by taking the god that the people worship and then take their resources such as gold, diamonds, oil and sometimes human beings.

Did you know that different areas have the system entity that they worship? Like China worships dragon. India worships snake and so many different areas worship different things as gods.

I established United Kingdom as a home of missionaries that will go and destroy all these energies and give **ME** glory, but what did Satan do? He said, 'oh so, **YOU** want to destroy me? Since **YOU** want to destroy me I will establish myself there.' And she cunningly established herself in the United Kingdom. Now as things are, the United Kingdom have a hand in feeding these gods. If they are, they should repent, **I** hope they are not. **MY** hand is not there. But **I** removed King James from there.

So, any day some people in United Kingdom takes their dragon back to China and took the egg of dragon from France to France, and returns the Egyptian mummy gods, back to

Egypt and returns serpent back to India, they would be free again. Apart from that they are still mixed up with **GOD** and evil.

Any country that is operating under the influence of negativism is a debtor to **THE ORIGINAL GOD**. As for individuals you have the right to worship the way you like. That is the reason freedom of worship was created in the whole world. You can worship anything you like, but at the end of the day we shall know who worships the **TRUE GOD, THE CREATOR OF THE UNIVERSE.**

After all these negative energies were brought into the United Kingdom, **I** left them partially and established America in the neck of the Indian Ocean, but the same problem arouse again. There is one family in California that was created that manifested through the Seer of the Seven Evil Angels that **I** deprived from coming back to Heaven, because of disobedience. That family that manifested from those Seven Evil Angels established the head of the human dragon there and started trouble. They also established the synagogue of Satan and mammon there to control money. All these things are to control money. What is this thing about?

Was that not the same thing that Satan took to Solomon when **I** made him King of Israel? And he used Queen Sheba for that.

What did Satan plan? He entered Pharaoh and said Solomon is too powerful. He is a powerful king and that will make people to only talk about Solomon, Solomon. So they sent Queen Sheba to use the money to go and bribe Solomon and control him. That was the plan of evil with Pharaoh.

Queen Sheba went there but this Sheba was a daughter of **GOD** and so she fell in love with the spirit of Wisdom being Solomon and so could not go ahead with the plan. She rather handed over all the wealth in the true heart to Solomon to use. But the problem was that Solomon had to pretend to bow down and did the ceremony of the god of fornication and prostitution and that was Sheba. God of money, mammon is generated by the energy of prostitution. That is why when you have sex in spirit soul, you are exploring money. That is exactly what it is. That was exactly what Satan did and that was what he said to Solomon of recent that since you do not want to explore that energy as the money then stay there. Let me see how you will manage but **I, THE FATHER GOD, AM** the one exploring Solomon now and

I have given Him the Wisdom of Riches, which is the positive one so all the **Mundane Kingdom, belongs to GOD.** Now the Kingdom of this world has become the Kingdom of Jehovah **GOD** and **HIS** Christ.

Queen Sheba died inside the temple of **GOD** of King Solomon of Israel, before the altar and she resurrected and from that day the power of the **Mundane World** belongs to **THE FATHER GOD** for eternity. In the name of our Lord Jesus Christ, Amen.

C: **THE MUNDANE OR ARTIFICIAL ARE LIFELESS**

Mundane or **Artificial** things are **lifeless** things. They have nothing to do with life or the soul. They are things that finish in this world. Do not therefore glorify in any of them. Do not fight for it. Do not struggle for it and do not trouble yourself for it, because you cannot take it to anywhere. Solomon said, "Vanity of vanities". That is the glory of the mundane world. It is not the Spirit of **GOD** that **GOD** gives to you, which you will take with you when you leave this world. Be you a President, Head of State, a King and Queen or have money, houses and all the beautiful things, your beautiful body as a man or woman or whatsoever all finish here. They end here. You cannot take them to anywhere, because they are artificial. They are not reality. Therefore, take it easy.

D: THE POWER OF MUNDANE AND THE CARNAL SUPREME FORCE ENERGY OF MONEY

The power that promotes the mundane world is money. Money was purposely created to use in controlling the whole world. It was to be that when the money is bulging in the pocket and does everything, nobody would be interested in **GOD** or anything spiritual. Why do people say, "There is no **GOD**?" They don't care. If you ask people these days to choose between these two: money or **GOD**. A lot of people will definitely choose money and leave **GOD** alone. They would reason thus: will I eat **GOD**?

Tell **ME,** who likes to suffer?
Who likes to live in a poor quality house?
Who likes to be without a car?
Who likes to suffer and stay without money?
Who likes to be without the conveniences of life and all the other beautiful things in the world?

That is the reason those serving Satan, the agents of Satan makes children of **GOD** to suffer and deprive them of these things if you don't sign up with them. If you do not join them, they make your life miserable so that you are forced to worship mammon, the artificial god of the world, which is evil.

Nonetheless, today as you know, since the **WORD** is everything they stand to lose. Well, the mistake they made is that they would have looked for a way to make these mundane things or money without the **SPOKEN WORD** but that is one thing they cannot do. How would they do that? The name money is the **WORD** therefore; **I AM THE OWNER OF MONEY.**

If you can do anything without the Spoken Word that means you can get that thing. Since **MY OWN** Energy, **MY SOUL** is the **WORD**, then **I AM** the only *ADAUSUNG, (IN CHARGE) and* **I AM** *dausong (charging)* everywhere, so money belongs to **ME.** The Word money belongs to **ME, I AM THE WORD**.

Okay take the money and give **ME** the **WORD** and see how it is going to work. You say oh this is secret society, this is Satan; this is evil. Take them and go, but give **ME** that

WORD and see whether that thing will exist again. That is **MY SUPREME** control!

If you read this information and you are a negative person, take your negativism and give **ME** the **WORD** that lives in you. Do not speak the Word again from that moment and see whether you will be happy.

As soon as you resume speaking the word or thought about the word, you have bowed down to the **Supreme WORD** of **GOD** and you have no excuse and no where to escape to.

So, **I THE FATHER GOD controls The Power of The Mundane and The Carnal Supreme Force of Energy of Money** now. And **I** will use them to make life easy for the whole world, but not to promote Satan or evil again.

E: WHAT ELSE CAN DESTROY HUMANITY APART FROM THE ARTIFICIAL OR MUNDANE GOD

The mundane god is money just like love is **GOD**, but they use fornication or sex as love. If you tell a woman – 'I love you', she will start thinking about fornication. Just go on the street, now and see a beautiful woman or man and say to her or him 'I love you too much.' Do you reckon the person would think oh let me forgive you your sins or you think the person would think you wanted something done for you or so? The person only has one thought in his or her mind.

'Do you have a woman?'

What has woman got to do with love?

'Do you have a man?'

What has man got to do with the Word **'love'**? That is the plan and handiwork of Satan, as negative, mistake and artificial.

With this artificial manner they made the word 'love' to be fornication while **LOVE** actually means **GOD**. The same thing is also with money because money is supposed to be the energy that controls the mundane world and to make life easy for everybody equally, but now do you see what they do? They do not distribute money in equal proportion to the whole inhabitants of the world as **I THE FATHER GOD** do with **The WORD.**

As **the WORD** lives in everybody's heart equally it is the same way that money should be in everybody's pocket equally. The government is supposed to share the money to everybody equally and what each individual does with his or her share is none of your business. If any can manipulate what they have well, they can do so.

Why did they have to make money to enter some hands, but block some people from getting it? They gave a name to it, but why should they do that. All that is the manipulation of the mundane energy system in the world and that is the system that destroys this world. For instance, everybody wants to live well and since you do not allow people to live well, they resort to theft. People can kill a fellow human being to take their money. If they know where money is housed they will burn down the place and take the money.

What causes all the problems in the world? It is money. You have elevated money more than **I THE FATHER GOD**.

You respect money more than **GOD**.

You worship money.

You adore money.

You treasure money and money has become **GOD** to you.

You have seen what money has done to you, your country and your family.

Money spoils the relationship between husbands and wives, spoils beautiful children with their parent and spoils this world.

Money is not Satan, but you use the love of money to spoil it, because without money you earn no respect. Without money you can't help your father, your mother and your child. You cannot give anything. Even in the church it is money first. Some say, if you do not have money don't come here, because **GOD** will not bless you as you have no money. Do you believe such church leaders to be true **GOD'S** servants or that he is a churchman? Of course he is working with the mundane system as an agent.

What is the meaning of being poor and being rich? If the government of the day is rich, everybody, **I** mean every citizen of that country should be a lucky person. Why are some people in that country poor and others rich? It means the spirit of **GOD** is not operating in that place. Why do some people live well and some others live impoverished lives, and the government exist in that place? So, what is the duty of the government? Does the government not belong to everybody?

The only thing that is for everybody is government. And the only thing that is for every child is mother and father. So, why should a country be rich and some people in certain parts of the country are poor? That should tell you that that country's administration is not from **GOD**. When you ask that they address the issue and remedy the situation, they point out to you that every finger is not the same.

Okay, every finger is not the same, but the fingers help one another, and they become equal. So why does you rich man not help a poor man? Why do you government not speak for the people that are not fairly treated? What is the duty of the government?

GOD'S Government is not yet established. That means the government of this world is the government of Satan as evil, because if the government of **THE FATHER GOD** were established they would behave as **GOD'S**.

Don't you know what **THE FATHER GOD** means? It means good, nice. **FATHER GOD** means equality, love, peace, and oneness! Don't you see that the government use law to control everybody? They ask you to pay tax. Under must, everybody must recognize government.

Government is supposed to make everybody in the whole world to respect, recognizes and worship **THE FATHER GOD THE CREATOR OF THE UNIVERSE** in spirit and in truth. Since no government in this world knows **THE FATHER GOD** do you see people take **THE FATHER GOD** as anything? That is the problem!

If **I** decide to do anything to this world, nobody should blame **ME, THE SUPREME WORD, THE DIVINE CREATOR**, because no government, no king, no prominent person, no rich and important person recognize **ME, THE FATHER GOD** as their Creator. Nobody worships **THE FATHER GOD** in a truthful way instead of that the so call poor human beings call the name of GOD just because they are poor, and as soon they become bless with a lots of money, they now go to meet evil people for protections.

This is the last chance **I** give to all governments, all human beings that they should celebrate **The Universal Supreme Word Season** and they should use the proceeds to balance out the differences of everybody's situation in this world. Without that you will answer **ME** who created this world and whether your government represents **ME, THE FATHER GOD** or not.

Or **I** will swear to **MYSELF, WORD** whether **I, THE CREATOR OF THE UNIVERSE** do not exist again? The **ONE** that dealt with people of old who deviated from the ordinance of **GOD**, like Pharaoh, like Nebuchadnezzar and the rest of the people that thought there was no **GOD**. And if the same

GOD still exists and kept quiet, then one day **I AM** going to prove **MYSELF, *same same now now be*,** in the name and blood of our Lord Jesus Christ. Amen.

F: THE WORD MUNDANE IS THE CARNAL ENERGY OF FORNICATION THAT PRODUCES ENERGY FOR THE MUNDANE SYSTEM

Everything in the world is fornication, which is the energy soul of the mundane system, and it belongs to human-animals and not human GODS. Indirectly, the majority in the world are trying to turn this world to be hell. As you are trying to turn this to be hell, that means animals are controlling you.

They established enforceable laws, but what shows that these laws are effective? They kill people anyhow. They do so many things anyhow. They only use laws to frighten innocent people, but these people do what they like.

With money people do what they like especially in Africa. Africa is not developed in understanding to know how to manipulate and use money like the Western World. The Western World is developed a way of using money now. They turned money to be god of the earth. They use it to make life easy. They use it to at least help some few people. But in Africa, someone will have money and bank the notes in his house until the money rots. He will not use it to do anything substantial and some of them would not even put them in the bank.

Someone has money and has ten cars and would not drive one car for one month. They would keep it covered in the garage or backyard. That is stupidity as an animal instinct! What do you do with all that? That is the wrong concept of using the mundane things.

The **mundane** thing was to maintain the physical creations. All these **mundane** things and **mundane kingdom** and things such as aeroplanes, cars and all, are not evil, but you use them to serve evil. Money is a very glaring example.

People say **GOD** does not want money and for that if you are a man of **GOD**, they take you away from the system. Anyone that is a preacher as **I AM** speaking this Word now people will dismiss as nonsense, because they reckon it has nothing to do with money.

Who tells you **GOD** is not money?
What is the Word?

"Abasi Mu-Udim" The Creator and Creations

What is the energy?

What is the idea of mundane?

Mundane Kingdom, Mundane glory means Sheba. Sheba means Mundane and Sheba now belongs to **GOD**.

When Abel died in the Garden of Eden, he died to procure the Mundane kingdom for **GOD** that is, minerals as the natural resources on earth. That was why when his Father was born, **HE** revealed to those wise men to take the mundane kingdom and surrender it to the Owner of the World, **THE CREATOR OF THE UNIVERSE**, which is The **WORD**. And now those who are as the three wise men are the people that will celebrate **The Universal Supreme Word Season,** because they know that the word is **GOD**.

I have now brought out the same test to the whole world. If you think you are a government, a business, a church, a mosque, a synagogue or anything that stands for Good and for positive actives then join King Solomon **ETE** in person. Make sure you follow Him to Celebrate **THE SUPREME WORD SEASON**. You should connect to Him and communicate with Him for the King Solomon Spiritual Library and follow the instructions to acknowledge yourself as a member of the **POSITIVE SUPREME WORD SEASON CELEBRATION, EVERY HUMAN BEING ARE CELEBRANT OF THE WORD BECAUSE I THE UNIVERSAL SUPREME WORD LIVES IN YOU**.

After you have done that demonstrate equality with your position, and then **I** will register you in spirit to be positive. Without that any second, any minute, any hour, any day, any week, any month, any year and any time **I** decide to destroy negativism, then you will be a part of it, just like Cain.

This is the remedy that **I** have used love to reveal today. So, **The WORD** controls the world of **mundane,** the carnal energy. And there is nothing you can do about it.

The Kingdom of this world belongs to Kingdom of **GOD** and HIS Christ. That is the meaning of it.

G: **THE WORD MUNDANE AND MONEY THE ARTIFICIAL PURSE OF CARNALITY, THE CARNAL ENERGY OF DEATH THAT STANDS FOR WATER**

Three part of the world is filled with water. That is why it seems that the Mundane Queendom or the Mundane Energy is trying to control the whole world, because the world is filled with mundane things. The world is full of fanciful and artificial things that man created and not the creations of **GOD**. However, when you create something there is energy in it. And the reason that energy rests on anything that man creates is, because man also is **GOD** since you use the **SPOKEN WORD**.

Everything that man creates is attached to an energy that can benefit another man, because you are the mini creator. That is what is happening today with this Revelation Lecture.

So water is causing problems for the blood and blood causes problems to the spirit. If the water and the blood surrender to the spirit, then every system of the human being is well and is without sickness. But any day the water insults the blood, the blood will have problems, which will affect the spirit. When the spirit leaves the body, the two of them as the water and the blood will end in that system and then who are you going to blame?

I AM the spirit that survives this world. You are concerned that the planet is abused and you chant the slogan, 'save the planet, save the planet!' Do you acknowledge **ME,** THE OWNER OF THE PLANET, THE SPIRIT THAT CONTROLS THE ATMOSPHERE when **I AM** THE ATMOSPHERE **MYSELF**?

If you really want to save the planet, control it and for there to be peace so that you live well, then you must recognize **ME, THE FATHER GOD,** the **ONE** that is talking these words, this particular **SUPREME WORD OF THE UNIVERSE.** When you recognise it you will see the difference in the universe. Without that, you should read the Lecture Revelation titled ***THE GREAT UNIVERSAL CHANGE*** to see what will happen in this world.

I have changed so many natures and so many planets in different areas. **I AM** cutting and joining and pasting the planets now and you will see what will happen.

Have you not seen why **I** created different areas with different atmospheres?

Some places are hot.

Some places are cold.

And in some places when the night comes that is when it is day time in other places and vice –versa.

I would have made every place look the same but **I** have done this to see the areas that will worship **ME** then **I** will focus attention on them and leave those that won't worship **ME** to suffer.

Now everybody says Africa is suffering. What makes Africa to suffer? Africa has nice weather all round because the weather of Africa is accurate. You need rain the rain falls. You need sun the sun shines. Everything you need is in normality. Green leaves from the beginning of the year to the end of year and that is the **Paradise of God**. If you see the whether not normalised anywhere in Africa then there is a reason why but it should not be so.

There are some parts of the world that during some months everything dies and that means that you only survive there in the mercy of **GOD** that **I** gave you, which you use to save the situation. However, any mistake and **I** tune it a little then you are finished, because you live in mundane manipulation.

You have buried electric wires everywhere. You have buried gas everywhere. Everywhere is artificial. And you are not sorry for yourself – artificial world?

So, do not allow too much artificial things and mundane things to enter your head, because they stand for destruction. Gas can burn down everywhere in this part of the world. If you put fire anywhere in Africa, it will burn for a tiny touch and go out, but if you put fire here in the United Kingdom or any part of the western world, it can burn to miles and miles and miles, because all the things are instruments for destruction for nature.

The reason earthquake is too much in the Western world is because they have dug undergrounds, undergrounds and more undergrounds everywhere. So, when one area collapses the rest follows and collapses into the water.

Do you know that I have a foundation stone in the ground that holds everything? But you drill and drill away deep into the ground. When you drill, drill and drill and the whole place collapses, whom will you blame?

Therefore, I do not want such a thing to happen to Africa. I put up barriers on lots of unnecessary development in Africa.

I want Africa to develop in love, in peace and so on. What I gave them is enough for them to generate a good life for everybody. It is not to build skyscrapers. Why not build bungalows.

Do you know why all these countries as America, China, Malaysia, United Kingdom and the rest of the countries of the world build skyscrapers? They are showing off and want to have a better view from their satellite. They want to do the exact thing they did in the Tower of Babel. What is the need for all that? Why not build small, small houses and live well? Anyway, partly but as secondary there is not enough land for simple buildings.

I have therefore, spoken **MY** mind and given these revelations today, but it is up to you to make good use of them.

The water disturbs the blood and the blood disturbs the air, which is the spirit and then **I** leave the body. But if the water as the carnal people behave well with blood as the natural people and the blood behaves well with the spirit as the spiritual people, there will be peace in this world, in the name and blood of our Lord Jesus Christ. Amen.

CONCLUSION A: **HE IS THE FATHER HE IS THE SPIRIT OF LIFE**

HE IS THE SPIRIT OF LIFE, HE IS THE FATHER GOD takes upper hand in everything on earth in spirit and in heaven. **HE IS THE FATHER** of the **SPOKEN WORD**. That is the reason all respect, all glory, all adornment, all recognition, all things should be via the **WORD, THE SUPREME WORD** to **THE FATHER GOD,** THE SPIRIT.

When you do this with humility and with love then you will know that **I, THE FATHER GOD,** THE SPIRIT has a representative in the soul, which is **THE SPOKEN WORD.** Through that **WORD** you know **THE FATHER** and through the **WORD** everything is created.

CONCLUSION B: **SHE IS THE NATURE OF BIRTH**

The Supernatural Nature as Natural is the Nature of Birth that is, the force of replanting and procreation. Nature brings procreation. Nature is the force of energy that multiplies things and camera things and brings them to physical being.

SHE IS THE MOTHER in **Nature.**
SHE IS THE MOTHER EARTH – natural.

Nature reproduces everything by the spirit of Nature. The work of Nature is to reproduce things while the work of Spirit is to create things to exist. When something exists in the as a shadow in the camera that is, in the soul, then the Nature takes it and multiplies it.

Nature is the Mother that produces things as birth. Natures stands for birth and it is **THE FATHER GOD** in Spirit of multiplication.

CONCLUSION C: **IT IS THE ENERGY OF DEATH**

Mundane things, **artificial** things and **money** are the **Energy of Death.** What causes problems is artificial energy.

So anyone that likes too much artificial, artificial, artificial ideas, artificial things as mundane things and worships and adores them has signed for death. When you die you will not germinate again.

A house has no child.

An aeroplane has no child.

A car has no child.

Anything mundane has no child.

Money has no child.

None of these things can reproduce. They only have one template that works in them, but they have no life. There is no energy of life in such things. There is no life in them. That is the meaning of death.

Artificial, mundane energy is death.

"Abasi Mu-Udim" The Creator and Creations

All artificial mundane energy should bow down to Natural things and respect natural things, which are the actual things.

Every birth in this world should be respected, whether a woman or a man, because that is the only thing that is alive. That is the only thing that is the biggest in life. Money and Man is equal in use, but they are not equal in respect and glory because LIFE as the WORD in man is greater.

Therefore, all mundane kingdoms and mundane things, no matter how big, should respect man that is, birth in Nature.

You build bombs but can they stand Nature? You can build anything as massive as massive can, as powerful as powerful can, and with the highest sophistication of technology but none can withstand Nature. One small wind, which is an angel, can destroy them within a twinkle of and eye.

So, you cannot fight Nature. Nobody can fight Nature. Mundane power cannot fight Nature. One thunder alone, or earthquake or fire and any small thing of Nature can destroy everybody. Even death can hamper things. If you go to sleep and never wake up again then that ends you and whatever plans that you intended to implement. So, respect the nature of birth, which is the energy of life **THE SPOKEN WORD.**

When these three things cooperate and are controlled by **THE FATHER GOD,** yet you do not respect **GOD** then, you are in trouble. That is what it is. **I, THE SPOKEN WORD** controls the energy of death and every thing that you call mundane in the world but all these things are artificial as money and all. So, if you misbehave and death acts in you and where you misbehave then that is the end of you and that place.

That is the Revelation Lecture of today, which is to reveal that **THE POWER AND THE ENERGY THAT CONTROLS EVERYTHING IS THE CREATOR AND THE CREATIONS, SPIRITUAL, NATURAL, MUNDANE OR ARTIFICIAL.**

Let those who have ears hear.

May **GOD** bless **HIS HOLY WORD** for every soul, now and forevermore, Amen.

In the name of our Lord Jesus Christ
In the Blood of Our Lord Jesus Christ
Now and forever more
THANK YOU FATHER!

Prayer by HRM Queen Disem Solomon David **ETE**:

Let thanks and praises be given to THE FATHER GOD in the name of our Lord Jesus Christ. Amen

Let thanks and praises be given to THE FATHER GOD in the name of our Lord Jesus Christ. Amen

Let thanks and praises be given to THE SUPREME NATURE OF THE UNIVERSE THE FATHER THE CREATOR OF THE UNIVERSE, now and forevermore. Amen

Holy, Holy, Holy

Thank YOU FATHER immensely for this wonderful Christ day once again for coming by thy self to give this recondite wisdom to all creations.

We thank YOU FATHER for coming to tell us what you spiritual base is and what thy nature is and also the mundane.

We thank YOU FATHER that through all this you've made us know that everything comes from THEE THE FATHER GOD. You are the Supreme Nature, the Administrator and if we wait for thy green light all will be well with us, now and forevermore. Amen.

Let thanks and praises be given to THE FATHER GOD in the name of our Lord Jesus Christ. Amen

Let thanks and praises be given to THE FATHER GOD in the name of our Lord Jesus Christ. Amen

Let thanks and praises be given to THE SUPREME WORD AND NATURE OF THE UNIVERSE THE TIME AND THE SEASON OF EVERYTHING, now and forevermore. Amen.

THANK YOU FATHER

Chapter Three

THE INSPIRATIONAL WRITER

KING SOLOMON SPIRITUAL LIBRARY
THE GOD ENCYCLOPAEDIA WORD OF INFINITY

INSPIRATIONAL WRITERS AND READERS OF THE
FATHER'S TALK
(GOD PRESENT)
KING SOLOMON SPIRITUAL LIBRARY

In the name of our Lord Jesus Christ In the blood of our Lord Jesus Christ Now and forever more, Amen

(A) REFERENCING THE FATHER'S TALK (GOD PRESENT) IN KING SOLOMON SPIRITUAL LIBRARY

I know some people will inspire when you visit King Solomon Spiritual Library website or bookshop, and have access to any of **THE FATHER'S TALK (GOD PRESENT)** information through books, electronics, audio and otherwise and are inspired to write or produce any information through the knowledge that you have gained, you must not fail to reference **THE FATHER'S TALK (GOD PRESENT)** in **King Solomon Spiritual Library** as the such of your inspirations.

(B) THE WORD OF TRUTH AND THE HOLY SPIRIT PRINCIPLES

Since **THE FATHER'S TALK (GOD PRESENT)** is the direct information from **THE FATHER GOD ALMIGHTY HIMSELF,** all positive children of God can be, and will be inspired with this **WORD** because the Word of **THE**

FATHER GOD, THE CREATOR OF THE UNIVERSE is a Spiritual Case Study for all souls to improve to have self awareness and a Higherself Consciousness.

When you are inspired and you want to write, make sure that your ideas, principles and concepts base on the Holy Spirit of Truth without changing the ordinance of the **FATHER'S TALK (GOD PRESENT).**

(C) THERE SHALL BE CONSEQUENCES THAT WOULD FOLLOW THOSE WHO USE THE MEANING, THE CONCEPTS AND THE PRINCIPLES OF THE FATHER'S TALK (GOD PRESENT) FOR THE PURPOSES OF MISLEADING

Consequences shall follow those who use the meaning, the concepts and the principles of **THE FATHER'S TALK (GOD PRESENT)** for the purposes of misleading in any manner.

Any Human-God, human-animal, human-bird or human-fish who has access to **THE FATHER'S TALK (GOD PRESENT)** through any means, be it via books, electronics, audio and otherwise should know that those words are not the words of human beings. The words are transcribed, proofread and accepted by **THE FATHER GOD** as it comes from the **SUPREME STUDIO OF THE ALMIGHTY FATHER GOD HIMSELF,** via **King Solomon Spiritual Library.**

When the signal of the information alerts HRM King Solomon David Jesse Etteh from **THE FATHER** through the **COMPREHENSIVE MEMORY OF GOD** in him, at anytime in the day or at night and anywhere, whether on the road or any public place, he will take note of the title of the Revelation Lectures. Sometimes if the location is conducive, lectures can take place immediately. If the location is not conducive, **THE FATHER** fixes the time for the full lecture to take place. Most of the time, some of the lectures take about a week, a month or six months and so on, to deliver when **THE FATHER** brings it back from **HIS SUPREME MEMORY** to HRM King Solomon Etteh.

Take note that the information of **THE FATHER'S TALK (GOD PRESENT)** is not preaching, or the giving of sermons or shared discussion. **THE FATHER** calls it *"LECTURE REVELATION"*, which is a Spiritual Case Study for mankind to improve and have the Higherself Consciousness about himself or herself and their creator.

For that reason, every human being that comes across any of this information of the **FATHER'S TALK (GOD PRESENT)** should treat it with utmost and absolute respect and reverence at all times.

HRM King Solomon David Jesse Etteh is not responsible for **THE FATHER'S TALK (GOD PRESENT)** but **GOD HIMSELF. THE ALMIGHTY FATHER** only uses him as a way through, just like a loud speaker from the radio or television receiver.

For this reason, HRM King Solomon David Jesse Etteh will not be held responsible by anyone who does not understand the contents, the concepts and the principles of **THE FATHER'S TALK (GOD PRESENT)** information in King Solomon Spiritual Library. He will not answer any questions or queries from spirit to soul and the physical truth in connection to the above from the lower mind individuals, persons or groups. However, if you are positive and you have love, you are humble, have patience and are peaceful and you want to know and understand more of any part of **THE FATHER'S TALK (GOD PRESENT); 'You should use fasting and prayer'** and or if anyone has any questions in good faith, he or she is free to write to HRM King Solomon and **THE FATHER** in him will respond. He will not, and there is no response to any questions, queries and anything negative with the craftiness of the evil minds of humankind.

That is why you should first read

THE FATHER GOD with **HIS SUPREME HOLY SPIRIT OF TRUTH** will bless all those who read and accept this information with good faith through the name and blood of our Lord Jesus Christ. Amen.

In the name of our Lord Jesus Christ
In the blood of our Lord Jesus Christ
Now and forever more, Amen

"THEUNISAL-SUREME SEACELION"
The Universal Supreme Season Celebration

"THEUNI-SUREME WORA THECRO-THEUNISE"
The Universal Supreme Word Almighty
The Creator Of The Universe

WWW.COME4WORD.COM

THE OFFICIAL SITE FOR

EVERLASTING UNIVERSAL ALL WORD SEASON APPRECIATION

"Abasi Mu-Udim" The Creator and Creations

CEREMONIAL PROGRAM

===========

THE UNIVERSAL SUPREME ALL WORD SEASON CELEBRATION

"Abasi Mu-Udim" The Creator and Creations

(GOD PRESENT)
SOMETHING MORE THAN
GOLD
IN THE HEART OF ALL MEN
IS THE
WORD

THE WORD IS THE MAKER, THE SOLE ADMINISTRATOR AND

THE CREATOR OF THE UNIVERSE.
THEREFORE, ALL MANKIND ON EARTH
MUST APPRECIATE
THE WORD IN ALL CAPACITIES FOREVER

═══════════════

FROM EVERY
OA OF AO TO AO OF AO
(1st OCTOBER TO 10th OCTOBER.)
YEARLY IS
THE UNIVERSAL SUPREME

ALL WORD SEASON

CELEBRATION TO APPRECIATE
THE FATHER GOD ALMIGHTY

CELEBRATION!
CELEBRATION!!

"Abasi Mu-Udim" The Creator and Creations

CELEBRATION!!!
THE UNIVERSAL SUPREME WORD CELEBRATION OF ALL TIME

=======

THE ALMIGHTY FATHER GOD, THE CREATOR OF ALL THINGS BROTHERHOOD

**ORGANISED BY
KING SOLOMON SPIRITUAL LIBRARY**

=======

HRM KING SOLOMON DAVID JESSE ETE

INSPIRATIONAL HEAD

IN THE HONOUR OF THE FATHER GOD THE CREATOR OF THE UNIVERSE THE HOLY SPIRIT OF TRUTH AND THE KING OF KINGS AND THE LORD OF LORDS

==========

THANK YOU FATHERo
KING SOLOMON SPIRITUAL LIBRARY

THE GOD ENCYCLOPAEDIA WORD OF INFINITY

==========

"Abasi Mu-Udim" The Creator and Creations

King Solomon Spiritual Library,
God Universal Information Centre
Father's Talk (God Present)

WITH LOVE

Covered: **This BOOK,** e-book, software or software's, books, website, video, audio, idea or ideas, formula or formulas, manual or instruction manual.

... Hereby gives you a non-exclusive license to use the ... (THIS BOOK). Some of the word here is coded with the (WORD OF SUPER HOLY AND INTELLIGENCE FATHER GOD ALMIGHTY)

Title, ownership rights, and intellectual property rights in and to the Website, Books, E-book, Audios and Videos, Shops and Store – e-Stores, Fundraisings, Celebrations and the supreme word seasons Celebration formulas and arrangement, Positive Inspiration, Holy (Fata), FATHER GOD ALMIGHTY POSSESSING SPIRIT in thought, in words and in did, thinking well, speaking well, hearing well and doing well shall remain in me and in ... The BOOK is protected by international copyright.

FATHER'S TALK (GOD PRESENT)
The message in The Father's Talk (GOD PRESENT) does not challenge any authority either individuals, groups or governments of any land or even any belief of any form. It is rather challenging the truth that is hidden from mankind. Therefore, any spirit, soul or physical human being who decides to challenge this truth shall have himself or herself to blame.

Key A
Any individual that reads any of The Father's Talk (GOD PRESENT) with faith; love and acceptance will experience immediate positive change in his or her

life from spirit, soul to physical. If he or she accepts the message then he or she will be free from any evil.

Key B: **PEACE AND LOVE**
If you do not believe the contents of any of The Father's Talk (GOD PRESENT) it is possible through The Father's divine love and peace simply hands over your copy to a friend or somebody else that would like to keep a copy, or signing out from any of the website that connected to The Father's Talk (GOD PRESENT) KING SOLOMON SPIRITUAL e-LIBRARY without any evil and negative comments and you are
blessed and free.

========

FROM THE DESK OF INSPIRATIONAL HEAD
Fees, Prices and Donations; There is no refund on fees, price or donations since your fees price or donations are using as a charity contribution to do administration work of THE SUPREME WORD, So

please kindly read this first before you decide to involves yourself in any of the under mention of HRM King Solomon David Jesse ETE universal Inspirational Businesses of (GOD PRESENT) in cash, kinds and otherwise.

I CAME FROM THE FATHER GOD, WITH THE FATHER GOD, AND BY THE FATHER GOD TO ESTABLISH THE FOLLOWING:

Therefore, all distributors and contributors of The Father's Talk (GOD PRESENT), The Spiritual Advice, Healing and Counselling on General Live (The Universal Supreme Spiritual General Hospital), New Songs and Psalms of King David and Solomon, The Word of **GOD** Processing City in Ikot Okwo or e-City online, The Trinity Celebration, **"OUC FUND"**, The Universal Bank Account For All Creations, **"ERUFA"** ETE Royal Universal Family, **"THEUNISAL-SUREME SEACELION"** The Universal Supreme Word Season Celebration To Appreciates THE FATHER GOD

ALMIGHTY "THEUNI-SUREME WORA THECRO-THEUNISE" The Universal Supreme Word Almighty, THE CREATOR OF THE UNIVERSE should attach this information to all readers, website visitors, distributors, affiliates person/group, celebrant and celebrations centres, supporters and promoters, members, workers and voluntary workers, Ete royal universal palace committee, governments and many other centres as an agreement. Please kindly know that I am not answering to any physical human except **PEACE, UNITY AND LOVE.**

"THEUNISAL-SUREME WORA THECRO-THEUNISE".

I AM IN THE STAGE OF SUPER HOLY AND INTELLIGENCE FATHER GOD POSITIVE MADNESS OF THE HOLY SPIRIT OF TRUTH,
ENYEN ODUDU ODUDU ODUDU ABASI MI OOO ZIM ZIM ZIM

ASSASU, POSITIVE POSITIVE POSITIVE. UKEMEKE AKA IDIOK UNAM.

Let the peace and blessing of the Holy Father abide with everybody who corporate with this divine Father's Talk (GOD PRESENT

THANK YOU FATHER

BY
THE HOLY SPIRIT OF THE FATHER GOD
THROUGH HIS SERVANT

Senior Christ Servant
HRM King Solomon David Jesse ETE
Brotherhood of the
Cross and STAR
Eteroyal Universal family
Ikot Okwo The Great City of Refuge, Ete Community
Ikot Abasi LGA-543001
Akwa Ibom State Nigeria-W/A
Tel. 08036693841
www.ksslibrary.com
Email: ksslibrary@eteroyalmail.com

READ AT LEAST SEVEN LECTURE'S REVELATIONS BEFORE YOU CAN MAKE ANY COMMENTS

In the Name of Our Lord Jesus Christ
In the Blood of Our Lord Jesus Christ
Now and forever more

Everybody should have access and read at least seven **FATHER'S TALK (GOD PRESENT)** Lecture's Revelations before you can make any comments about it. If you do not go through at least seven **FATHER'S TALK** lectures and you comment you may make mistakes. When you make mistakes your blood will be upon you because you would have taken voluntary evolution to misquote **THE FATHER GOD THE CREATOR OF THE UNIVERSE.** If however, you go

through any seven of **THE FATHER'S TALK (GOD PRESENT)** –
one of **THE FATHER'S TALK** stands for one Spirit of God, which means that **FATHER'S TALK GOD PRESENT** Lectures Revelation are witness by the Seven Spirits of God, which **I** use as the Seven Church of God and Seven days of the Week, Seven spirits of Creations in one Supreme energy of THE FATHER GOD, THE SPOKEN WORD.
When you read seven **FATHER'S TALK** Lectures then, **I THE FATHER GOD** will reveal you as positive person. Then you will have a portion in **ME**. One of **THE FATHER'S TALK** will have a portion in you. Then you would know that this information came from **THE FATHER GOD.**
The Father's Talk God Present is not a mere talk from a man!
In the Name of Our Lord Jesus Christ
In the Blood of Our Lord Jesus Christ
Now and forever more
WWW.THEWORDCITY.COM

www.ksslibrary.com

THE UNIVERSAL SUPREME ACKNOWLEDGEMENT

'THE ONLY SOURCE AND REMEDY
TO END ALL HUMANITIES PROBLEMS'

Join me to Celebrate;
Acknowledge,
Appreciates and give full
RECOGNITION to
THE UNIVERSAL SUPREME WORD,
YOUR LIFE FORCE,

> **THE TOTALITY OF ALL TOTALITIES**
> **YOUR CREATOR,**
> **THE FATHER GOD ALMIGHTY,**
> **THE CREATOR OF THE UNIVERSE**

WWW.COME4WORD.COM
Contact EMAIL:
hrmkingsolomon@eteroyalmail.com

THANK YOU FATHE

================================

ESTABLISH MY SPIRITUAL LIBRARY

I THE FATHER GOD ALMIGHTY THE SUPREME WORD OF THE UNIVERSE AM THE SPIRITUAL FOOD TO FEED YOUR SOUL. Therefore, I want every family in this world, every home in this world, every office, government offices, monarchies, countries, states, regions, counties, communities, local authorities compound, family homes, everyone everywhere should be collecting published copies of **THE EVERLASTING GOSPEL AND THE FATHER'S TALK (GOD PRESENT)** Lectures Revelations of KING SOLOMON SPIRITUAL LIBRARY should be established physically in your houses. So that everybody should have those RECORDS. Go to read the books regularly. Every family should have this Library **MY INFORMATION CENTRE** for their family members.

Every generation of the particular family could easily go to their family Library of KING SOLOMON SPIRITUAL LIBRARY EVERLASTING GOSPEL and the **FATHER'S TALK (GOD PRESENT) Lectures Revelations** and read the Gospels and Lectures Revelations. Generations upon generations will access their KING SOLOMON SPIRITUAL LIBRARY.

You must all have **THE LIBRARY OF THE FATHER GOD ALMIGHTY** called **KING SOLOMON SPIRITUAL LIBRARY FATHER'S TALK (GOD PRESENT) LECTURES REVELATIONS** in your homes and offices. The authorities and individuals concerned must see to that. When you establish your branch of KING SOLOMON SPIRITUAL LIBRARY and have Everlasting Gospels and the **FATHER'S TALK (GOD PRESENT)** Lectures Revelations that place is blessed and secured. In the name and Blood of Our Lord Jesus Christ, now and forever more. Amen.

THANK YOU FATHER

==========================

The title List of some of the
Father's Talk
(GOD Present)

1: THE MANUAL OF THE SPOKEN WORD

2: THE MANUAL OF LIFE

3: INVESTMENT WITH GOD

4: ISO IBOT EDEM IBOT

5: THE CHARACTER OF THE NEW WORLD

6: HELPMANTRANS

7: UNDERSTANDING MY WORD

8: TRUTH, POSITION, POST AND NAME

9: NON STOP BLESSING

10: IMPRESSION

11: STAGES OF EDUCATIONS (SPE, SSE & SUE)

12: THE ENGINEERING OF LIFE

13: THE CONTENT PACKAGE

14: THE BUDGET OF THE NEW WORLD

15: DIVINE ATTENTION

16: THE BABY SPIRIT

17: PROMOTION

18: ADVANCE AND PROGRESSING MIND

19: THE TEMPLE OF THE LIVING GOD

20: I AM OK

21: THE SPIRIT OF TRUTH

22: THE PERFECT PERMANENCY

23: THE FATHER GOD, GOD, GOD THE FATHER

24: HUSBAND, WIFE AND CHILD

25: GOD AND HIS HARBINGER

26: LIFE EVERLASTING

27: POSSESS

28: MY MIND AND MY PLAN

29: AFTER HEART AND AFTER MIND

30: MY DECLARATION & STAND IN BCS

31: BEYOND THE HOPE OF FAITH

32: MENTAL STAIN

33: THE PRINCIPLE OF SELF HOLD

34: THE MASTERSHIP

35: HIDU-CUM

36: THE UNIVERSAL PARENT

37: ADVANCED YOU AND ME

38: THE GREAT UNIVERSAL CHANGE

39: THE PROJECTED MIND
40: INDESTRUCTIBLE BLESSED FIVE STARS

41: ASTROTS, GOD PRESENT I AND MY FATHER

42: SONGS THE COMPLETION

43: THE RIGHT BUTTON

44: AKWA ABASI IBOM- ETE - DIRECTING NDITO AKWA IBOM

45: THE DIGITAL AGE

46: GOD IS OFFICIAL CHAMPION

47: A TRUE WITNESS

48: MYSTERY OF PROCREATION AND BIRTH

49: THE UNIVERSAL UMBRELLA

50: THE FORERUNNER

51: <u>A OF A TO Z (FIRST OF ALL)</u>

52: MAN IN THREE CAPACITIES

53: THE TRUE LIFE OF HOLY SPIRIT PERSONIFIED

54: IN-BETWEEN THE FATHER & THE SON

55: DIVINE ARRANGEMENT & AUTHORITY

56: TWENTY FIRST CENTURY IS NOT FOR SATAN

57: THE SUPREME WORD SEASON CELEBRATION

58: THE MAXIMUM DEITY

59: TRANSFORMER TRANSMITTER AND WAVE

60: THE SUPREME FUTURE

61: THE BYLOVE OF WORD

62: THE SIGNATURE OF THE FATHER GOD

63: THE TWO WAYS

64: THE UNDERSTANDING OF LIFE

65: THE GREATER THAN SOLOMON IS HERE

66: THE CONQUEROR

67: THE SPIRITUAL GENERAL INSPECTOR OF LIFE

68: THE NIGERIA IN THE AFRICA Part one

69: THE NIGERIA IN THE AFRICA Part two

70: <u>THE CREATOR AND CREATIONS PART ONE</u>

71: THE CREATOR AND CREATIONS PART TWO

72: THE CREATOR AND CREATIONS PART THREE

73: THE SUPREME TEACHER

74: THE SPIRITUAL COVER

75: THE NIGERIA IN THE AFRICA PART THREE

76: THE SUPREME BELIEVE

77: CAST AND BAN (LECTURE IN LIVERPOOL)

78: LIFE EXTENSION MANUAL

79: THE SPIRITUAL TRAFFIC

80: THE VOICE OF THE CREATOR

81: MY OFFICE

82: LIFE SPIRITUAL FIRE EXTINGUISHER

83: INFORMATION

84: FATHER GOD FINAL ARRANGEMENT

85: THE LOVERS OF CHRIST

86: I LOVE YOU, I LOVE YOU TOO

87: THE UNIVERSAL SUPREME UPDATE

88: THE SUPREME ALTAR

89: THE SOURCE AND DESTINATION

90: A SON LIKE THE FATHER THE KING OF KINGS A ROOTS FROM HEAVEN (NOT THIS TIME AROUND)

91: THE TRUE WITNESS AND THE TRUE SERVANT

92: THE FINAL ARRANGEMENT

93: A TRUE NIGERIAN MAN AND WOMAN

94: EVERYONE MUST PERSONALLY INVOLVE

95: BEWARE

96: ESIEN EMANA AKPAN "THE AFRICAN PROBLEMS"

97: THE SECRET OF THE UNIVERSAL PROBLEMS AND THE REMEDY (MUSLIM AND CHRISTIAN FROM THE SAME PARENT)

98: <u>MMU-UDIM – THE BLESSED MOTHER (ABASI ME UDIM)</u>

99: THINK WELL, SPEAK WELL AND DO WELL

100: THE STAGES OF HOW TO PROCESS THE WORD

101: EVIL STAIN, WHO RUNS AWAY FROM WHO

102: BEYOND HUMAN KNOW PURELY SPIRITUAL

103: THE INSPIRATIONAL WRITER

104: BIAKPAN OBIO AKPAN ABASI (THE NEW JERUSALEM CITY)

105: "OBAMA" THE STRAINTHEN AND THE SPIRIT OF BILL GATE AND MICROSOFT

THANK YOU FATHER

www.ingramcontent.com/pod-product-compliance
Ingram Content Group UK Ltd.
Pitfield, Milton Keynes, MK11 3LW, UK
UKHW041258180426
11947UKWH00008B/549